NIGHT RUNNING

NIGHT RUNNING

A BOOK OF ESSAYS ABOUT BREAKING THROUGH

WELLSTONE BOOKS

WELLSTONE CENTER
in the Redwoods

Book Design: Alicia Feltman of Lala Design
Cover Design: Alicia Feltman

Printed in the United States of America

FIRST EDITION ISBN 978-0985419073

Wellstone Books is an imprint of the Wellstone Center in the Redwoods
858 Amigo Road Soquel, CA 95073

Distributed by Publishers Group West

TABLE OF CONTENTS

1. On Not Running at Night BY EMILY MITCHELL ... 1

2. This One's for You, Mom BY JOY RUSSO-SCHOENFIELD ... 11

3. Chasing Shadows Through the Night BY ANNE MILLIGAN ... 23

4. Off the Trail With Forty-Seven Miles to Go BY PETE DANKO ... 37

5. The Land of the Midnight Sun BY VANESSA RUNS ... 51

6. Alone With the Dinosaurs in East Berlin BY STEVE KETTMANN ... 61

7. Running to the Interior BY DAHLIA SCHEINDLIN ... 71

8. Escaping an Intervention BY HEATHER SEMB ... 81

9. One Headlight: Finding My Stride Along the Palisades BY T.J. QUINN ... 91

10. Lost in the Thai Countryside BY KELSEY EILAND ... 109

11. Beginner's Mind BY BONNIE D. FORD ... 117

EMILY MITCHELL, author of the novel *The Last Summer of the World* and, most recently, *Viral: Stories*, teaches at the University of Maryland and lives in Washington, D.C.

1

ON NOT RUNNING AT NIGHT

BY EMILY MITCHELL

*W*hen I first started running, I almost always ran at night. In Virginia, in the summer, the heat and humidity were too intense to run in the day. So I would wait until the sun went down, then go out on the still cooling sidewalks where fireflies filled up the trees with migratory lights. The suburbs had scraped the landscape of almost all its forest, but some patches of woods had been left, sad islands, and animals moved between these hiding places at dusk. Sometimes I saw deer lope across a road, silhouettes against the lit-up yards or caught in the circle of a streetlamp, turning their long necks to look at me with eyes the color of oil. More rarely, I saw the mirror-eyes and quick passage of a fox. The trees shivered with the dry clicking of cicadas, the grass of the tidy, chemical lawns creaked with crickets. I would glimpse these things as I moved past them, staying with them for a second. Then a moment later both of us would be gone.

I liked to be out at night when the streets were empty and to see these things that other people, inside their houses, didn't see. From the windows came the blue of television screens, the bright yellow lights of kitchens, each house its own world unaware of anyone outside it, seeing. I was fifteen years old, my family had just ambivalently emigrated from Britain and I had started running because I wanted to be thin, something which my new school and new country seemed to feel was important for a girl. I had tried to give up eating, first selectively, making an ever longer list of forbidden foods, then completely, which should have been simple, right? I just wouldn't eat at all and that would transform me from an awkward, bookish, serious girl with funny-looking clothes into a sociable and well-liked beauty. Not eating, however, was much more difficult than I'd anticipated and didn't in any case have the desired effect; it just made me hungry, dizzy and cranky. I had seen top runners on television, and they were all very slender and tall just like I wanted so badly to be, and I thought that perhaps if I did what they did, I would look like them. I ran around the suburban development where my family lived every day with that earnest dedication of which certain teenage girls are capable. I ran for miles. My body, of course, remained more or less the same shape it had been since puberty, round and pear-shaped – the same shape that it is today.

But something I did not expect also happened: I discovered that I liked to run for its own sake. Moving through the blue of early night, I would settle into my body's actual size and shape, its frame of bones and circuits of muscles and blood, its rhythm of breath. I would feel its strength and because of the combination of darkness and motion, some of the terrible self-consciousness that I felt the rest of the time would go away. I would relax. I would feel at home and graceful in the world, comfortable with my place in it, outside looking in, nearly invisible, observing, noting, standing back from things to see them: the position, not coincidentally, of both the runner and the writer.

The discovery of this refuge helped me survive the rest of high school and helped when I moved again, this time to go to college in Middlebury. Running was a companion, as it has been ever since in my highly transient life. It was something stable and dependable, something the old place and the new one could have in common. At school, it was a way for me to get away from the constant presence of other people, roommates and friends, and be by myself. It was a way to explore my surroundings, to learn the shape of the new place, to clear my head. I ranged farther than I could have as a pedestrian but without the shell that keeps drivers from being exposed to their surroundings. This combination gave me a feeling of freedom because I could go anywhere I wanted.

I ran at dusk along the shoulders of the country roads that led away from the campus. The bands of blacktop rose and fell with the landscape and I could see them stretching away towards the next crest or curve as I followed them. I would see cars approaching from far off, two headlights plowing through gathering gloom, the sound of the engine beginning far away like the sound of an insect, then growing closer. I would imagine who was in the car, where they were going, imagine how they saw me by myself out in the open space. In the spring, the fields smelled of manure, the verges turned green from winter gray. In the fall, the trees were delicate, fiery colors covering the hillsides. As dark descended, lights came up on the buildings of the college and the town beyond it, creating halos that made me feel lonely but also comforted, because I knew, or thought I knew, that I would not be outside like this for long. I was always aware that being out in the world alone, especially at night, carried its share of risk.

The next place I lived was Japan, in the suburbs of Osaka, where I went to learn the language while still a student. There I ran along narrow streets with no space for sidewalks. The walls of the houses came right up to the road, because space was so scarce and valuable, and where there weren't houses there were reinforced concrete embankments to keep the hillsides from collapsing beneath the weight of buildings piled on top of them. In other places, there were drainage ditches right beside the road for the rain to collect in. So I ran in a narrow margin between walls and traffic.

I didn't mind this. I needed more than ever the space and solitude that running gave me. I was conspicuous when I ran, relatively tall and white and red-haired, but I was conspicuous all the time in Osaka. Like most foreigners, I was followed by children shouting "Hello, hello" just to see if I'd react.

One evening, while I was out running, I heard the high growl of a motorcycle engine approaching from behind me. Lots of people, mostly men, rode motorcycles in Japan. The *bosozoku* motorcycle gangs would ride through the streets at night, slowly, in formation, all gunning their engines at once so that they sounded like a swarm of angry, giant bees. This engine sounded high and loud, approaching fast but then its note began to drop as if it were slowing down. I saw its headlights sweep the street ahead of me and approach, passing me, too close, I thought, and I was about to turn so I could see where it was and get out of the way if necessary. Then suddenly I felt someone reach out and slide a hand between my legs.

In another second, the driver had sped up again and was gone. He was down the street and out of sight before I'd really had a chance to even fully register what had taken place. I had never been touched without my own consent before and for a moment, I was utterly confused, convinced that I must know this person, that this must be a friend playing a prank, although what on earth the joke could be I did not know. Another few seconds and I understood what had happened and a wave of absolute anger rose up my chest. I sprinted uselessly down the street trying to get the driver back in view, with the idea that I could write down his license plate number and take it to the police. The next moment my anger was replaced by a sick feeling because I had done nothing to defend myself. I thought: If only I'd turned around and knocked him off his bike, if only I'd turned around to face him, he would not have been able to do what he did. But I didn't do any of that. I didn't do anything at all. I just stood at the side of the street, and watched his taillight disappear into the distance and then walked home, through streets which no longer seemed like a refuge from anything.

★ ★ ★ ★ ★

After that I didn't go running at night for a long time. In part this was a response to what happened in Japan. Also, for many years, I lived in cities where it did not seem prudent to be out at night by myself in the kind of isolated places where running sometimes took me. Instead, I ran during the day.

In London, where I got a job at a magazine after graduating college, I ran circuits around Finsbury Park. In the early mornings, there were other people running, but the grass was often covered with the remains of late-night, park-bench boozing, human and otherwise. Once I stopped because I thought that there was a dead body on the grass: an old man in grim clothing, gray pants and an overcoat that looked like a large fungus, his face immersed in beard. I remember that I was worried about what to do, whether I should touch him to see if he was still alive or whether I should just go to a phone and dial the emergency services (this was the 1990s and there were still pay phones). I was just about to go and call someone, when he grunted and rolled over, put his hands beneath his head and curled his legs up, into the position of a sleeping child. Another time, I was stopped by some girls who told me that their church could cure people of AIDS and invited me to come to services there. Yet another time, a man sitting on a bench made clicking noises at me as if I were a wandering pet dog.

After London, I lived for seven years in New York City, moving back home initially for a relationship that did not last, then staying because I had learned that, like it or not, I am American. When I lived in Queens, I ran towards the East River through the streets of Astoria, past stores selling groceries from Greece, Cyprus and Croatia, North African tea shops with sidewalk tables where men sat smoking hookahs, stores selling clothing with faked labels, dollar stores. Sometimes, men would comment and catcall as I went past.

"Can I come jogging with you?" someone asked once.

I could not avoid passing men by in the shared space of the streets, so I braced when I approached them. I wore old, loose clothing but it didn't make any difference. Just to be out, to be moving, was enough to bring on the attention. I bought an iPod and sunglasses, which allowed me to pretend not to hear. When I reached the river, I turned and ran along the bank, up towards Hell Gate Bridge, where when the tide was out in the estuary I could hear the chiming of thousands of worn pieces of colored glass turned over by the small waves that lapped the shore. Then I circled back along residential streets of terraced, brick houses with vinyl awnings over the windows, front yards surrounded by waist-high chain-link. In one yard there was a statue of the Virgin Mary with her arms open like a conductor before the musicians begin. In another, plastic windmills in the flowerbeds.

After that, living in San Francisco, where my fiancé had a fellowship, I ran from the Mission along 16th Street. It was the only flat route in the city so I doubled back on myself. I crossed under the 101 and up past the Giants' ball park until I reached the bay. Then I went around the edge of the peninsula past the Ferry Building until I reached the hoardings for the Teatro Zinzanni, which showed the giant faces of the circus performers, covered in white makeup and exaggerated pantomime expressions of surprise and delight. People sat and watched the bay or slept on the benches with their belongings all around them. Other people sat outside restaurants and drank brightly colored cocktails or ate food from large, white plates. Out over the blue water, seagulls swooped and turned.

I discovered that running itself is a kind of dusk. You

are between states and places; you are present, but you are simultaneously departing. You see things that other people miss and have time to observe them. In daily life, most of our traveling is done in haste and with a goal and a destination in mind. When we run, we emerge into the world with movement itself as the purpose. The state of mind of the runner, as of the city-walker, the *flaneur*, is more like the state of mind of the dreamer: the connections between what you encounter are spatial and sensory, not rational. It is the kind of experience we often have only or primarily at night.

Perhaps for this reason, I missed running at night through all the years I didn't do it. I had memories – the feeling of the cool and the dark, the air on my skin – that persisted and did not seem to fade or go away even after years had passed. Then, two years ago, I moved with my husband to Cleveland, this time for my work, teaching at a university there. In the evenings, in summer, the streets in the old, streetcar suburb where we live are cool and pleasant. The enormous trees rustle and move. And I noticed, shortly after our arrival, that there were many runners out on the nighttime roads.

In the area where we live, most of the buildings date from the 1920s, when the city was at its most prosperous, a rival to Chicago. These houses are all built to look like something else: a Tudor country inn, an English stately home or a French chateau. The houses are still grand, but the area is depopulating as people leave to follow the jobs that have already left; many of them are empty, abandoned or for sale. At night these empty buildings make patches of deeper darkness between the window lights around them.

Running at night here, you see clearly the vacancy the city suffers from, how many people have left and what that looks like. There are animals: rabbits that bolt frantically when I get close, giving themselves away, and skunks and deer and even sometimes bears, although fortunately I haven't met one of these yet when I'm out by myself on a long stretch of sidewalk. When I am out running at night I'll sometimes meet another runner coming in the opposite direction and we will nod or wave or mouth hello. Then we'll return to our separate solitudes as we move on. I carry a cell phone with me just in case. I don't often feel anxious when I'm out at night, although I am aware that I am making a choice to be unseen and alone and that this is not a choice that everyone would make. So I go out, begin to run, become aware of my body and my limbs, which are almost the only things I've brought with me, for better or worse, through all these different places. Then as I hit my stride, I find myself in the space that I discovered all those years ago, where I am clear and invisible at the same time.

JOY RUSSO-SCHOENFIELD, a former writer and editor at the *Palm Beach Post*, *Newsday* and CBS Sportsline.com, oversees Olympics and international sports coverage for ESPN digital and print media. She lives in Burlington, Connecticut.

2

THIS ONE'S FOR YOU, MOM

BY JOY RUSSO-SCHOENFIELD

The headlamp was just sitting there, peeking out from under a pile on the kitchen counter. For almost three weeks I'd left it lying amid the usual collection of keys, bills and spare change, after a friend had lent it to me to try out. I was tired of wondering if I would ever have the nerve to put the thing to use. So one night without thinking too much, I told myself this was as good a time as any to take the plunge, and threw on my gear, pulled the headlamp down into place and waved goodbye to my husband and dog.

"If I am not back in forty-five minutes, send the search party," I called over my shoulder on my way out the door.

Our long driveway was icy enough that I left nothing to chance. I hopped into the car and drove down to the foot of the driveway before I started my run, naked. No music, no Nike+, just me and the road. My lungs slowly adjusted to the cold, which turned out to be bearable. The crunch of the salt and sand under my feet felt right, assuring, offering stability and traction. All I had to do was follow the bobbing light. Sounds hit me with an exaggerated clarity I somehow found comforting. A dog, confined by its humans' house, barked and scratched from behind a door. A tree creaked. Melting snow trickled into gutters.

With each step of the two-and-a-half-mile run, my senses became even more focused. A car threatened to encroach on my space, but with hearing hyper-alert it gave itself away long before I saw it. I heard rustling in the distance, then a howl farther away. Salt dust kicked up from the winter-worn roads, but I cut through it like a ghost.

It was as if my mind were set on shuffle mode, bouncing all over the place. Like the homing pigeons that lived on my grandfather's rooftop coop in Brooklyn, my thoughts worked their way backward, from my disbelief that I was actually out running in the dark to a sudden focus on what pushed me to get out there and put one foot in front of the other in the first place. I heard myself saying, out loud: "I'm sorry."

★ ★ ★ ★ ★

All of a sudden everything started moving in slow motion. I was perfectly positioned, for once, to stop my big brother Charles from scoring in our weekly deck hockey league. I was in the slot, or as much as I could make out of the slot from the beat-up high school tennis courts we were playing on. He was winding up to take his shot, which sent the bright orange-colored rubber ball straight to my inner left thigh. I knew it was coming, and I didn't care. I was going to stop the shot. I was going to be Adam Graves. I was going to be the hero.

My body blocked the shot, and I cleared it out of the zone. Victory. Even better – Charles smiled and chuckled under his breath. He was proud of me. I was beaming. On the car ride home, the three of us – Charles, my other brother Jeff and me – guzzled Gatorades and replayed all of our favorite moments. Jeff turned to ask me something, but before he could get the words out his eyes grew wide.

"Look at your leg!"

Just below my Umbro shorts line, an apple-sized bruise was about three shades of blue and red.

"Awesome!" I cried, thrilled.

"But you know someone who is not going to be happy," Jeff warned.

"*Charles! Jeff! What did you do to your sister?!*" Charles belted out in a high-squealed impersonation of our mother's Brooklynese.

We all howled with laughter, knowing full well how much truth there was to the joke. I didn't make it five feet past the front door before my mother weighed in.

"What happened to you?" she interrogated me, then switched her focus to my brothers. "What did you *do* to her?!"

"Mom, really, I am fine," I said. "I blocked Charles' shot. It helped win the game! It's just a bruise."

"Just a bruise!"

She let her outrage sink in.

"If it hit you just a little higher or lower, who knows what would have happened?" she continued.

"She'd have a bruise on a different part of her leg?"

Charles shot back.

"Don't get smart, Charles," Mom scolded.

"Well, just because it's something *you* would never do doesn't make it a bad thing," I said, feeling my joy slipping away quickly. It would shift into a defensive impatience and, finally, anger. I knew this drill.

"Joy, you could have hurt yourself."

"So what if I did? I don't care. It was fun. I blocked a shot like Adam Graves."

Like Adam Graves? That was too much for my mother.

"Those are hockey players," she said. "You're just a ..."

I cut her off before she could do more harm.

"Whatever!" I said. "It will go away. *You* would have never done it."

I hurried off to my room and pulled the door shut behind me.

★ ★ ★ ★ ★

My father was an all-city high school basketball player in 1950s Brooklyn, and I fondly remember him playing well into his fifties, against guys half his age, just waiting for them to call him "old man" so he could shut them all up with his deadly outside shot. He never gloated, he just smiled as he ran back down the court.

Surely this competitive drive was something he could have passed on to his daughter, as he did to my two older brothers. Unfortunately, no. This was the man who was afraid to pick me up as a baby out of fear that lifting me from underneath my arms would affect my, um, chest development. (My brothers and I still joke about how we are all still waiting for "the talk" from either of our parents.) When I recently asked him why he never took me out onto the court as a kid or signed me up for a youth sports league, he searched for words to try to explain.

"I don't know," he said. "It wasn't intentional. I just thought that wasn't something little girls did."

As for my mother, well, Rosemary didn't like exercise or sweating. The only time I can recall her and I ever engaging in any kind of physical activity together was shortly after our family made the move from Long Island to South Florida. My father was sick of winters and two-hour-long commutes on the Long Island Railroad, so we took the plunge into the sunshine. To take advantage of the warmer climate, and perhaps make a few new friends, my mom signed us both up for tennis lessons at the local country club. She lasted a few months before she gradually stopped going. I continued to play during summer camp, but the lessons stopped.

Mom also started to smoke again on the sly about five years after overcoming breast cancer and the double mastectomy and reconstructive surgery that followed. (She did eventually quit, once and for all, before I finished elementary school.) She was into those Jane Fonda workouts for a while, as most women of a certain age were in the mid–1980s. (Those leg-warmers!) As soon as I would hear "Can You Feel It" from the Jacksons blast out of the VCR, I'd run to join her. She never seemed to be having fun, though, and that workout routine soon enough faded away, like the others.

I swam a lot, and loved it, but never took formal lessons.

I dreaded PE at school. And the nights before the Presidential Fitness Tests were the worst. We had to run a mile in under twelve minutes and I always made it just by a nose. We also had to do pull-ups in front of the whole class, a move I have still not mastered to this day, probably because I can still hear the kids laughing at me. Softball also made me break out in cold sweats because the toughest girl in school was always on my team and she wore these cut-off gloves that were cool and menacing at the same time. I tried to talk to my mother about such insecurities, and it never went well.

"Oh, you poor thing!" she would say. Or, even worse: "Do you want me to call the school and talk to your teacher?"

I dreamed that Shirley MacLaine's "Aurora" from *Terms of Endearment* would take over my mother's body and yell out, "Don't worry! You're fan-fucking-tastic!" Was that asking too much?

It's all about who you know at that age. When a few of my friends suggested I come with them for cheerleading tryouts, my thought was: *Are there pull-ups involved? No? OK, what do I have to lose?* I made the sixth-grade squad and was a cheerleader all through junior high and high school. Cheerleading gave me something to be part of. My parents even approved, especially Mom. She loved the uniforms, except the one-shoulder number I wore senior year.

Cheerleading also kept me in shape. We were more of a competition squad, as most are in Florida, so we did plenty of stretching and jumping and tumbling. (I only landed a back handspring twice.) My arms were ripped and I was dubbed "Beast Woman," because at a whopping five feet five inches and a hundred and twenty pounds, I was too big to be thrown in the air. So I reveled in my "base" role and tried to be a good teammate, not always easy within the gaggle that is fifteen teenaged girls.

Once cheerleading ended with high school graduation, I was physically lost. No one ever prepared me for the Freshman Fifteen. I'd go to the gym, but I didn't know how to pace myself. I didn't know how to balance out my diet. I thought my high school habit of weekly trips to McDonald's for a Quarter Pounder with Cheese and fries wouldn't catch up to me. But of course it did.

Life was catching up to my mother as well. During my junior year of high school, she had to have a hysterectomy. Her surgeon blamed it on two miscarriages and three C-sections that had left her with numerous internal adhesions and scar tissue. But the surgery brought little relief. Instead, my mother later developed interstitial cystitis, a bladder pain syndrome that eventually forced her to go on long-term disability and kept her bedridden for weeks at a time.

I was not used to seeing her this way. Locked out from the one part of her life that brought her constant confidence, her job as an executive assistant, she was emotionally lost and quickly dipped into depression. That led to therapy, which led to Prozac, and this was back in the early days of Prozac, when it was conveniently available but not well understood. My mother was not the same person. She was irritable and sometimes irrational. I already tended to be on pins and needles around her, not wanting her to baby me about anything, but now I was truly dumbfounded.

One time when I was seventeen she screamed at me because – she insisted – I was poking potatoes the wrong way before putting them into the oven. I laughed and put the potatoes on the counter.

"You do it, then," I told her.

I knew it was the drugs talking, but I couldn't help reciting my internal mantra anyway: "I don't want to be like her!"

★ ★ ★ ★ ★

By the time I hit my mid-thirties I was seventy pounds from my cheerleading days, and work stress was beginning to take a toll. I loved my job, but it was the only thing I loved, outside of my husband and family and friends. I knew I had to find a way back to moving my body, so I signed up at a local YMCA and went online to soak up as much information as I could on training and nutrition. Yoga, my saving grace, taught me how to breathe. Indoor triathlons were an interesting experiment, but not more than that. Fortunately, some friends from work began weekly walks, and one of our outings evolved into half-walking, half-jogging at a local reservoir trail. That in turn led, amazingly enough, to my being able to run the whole 3.4-mile loop. Before long I entered my first 5K, then a 10K and, miraculously, my first half-marathon.

Once running is part of your life, if you are truly doing it for yourself and no one else, then nothing will get in the way of hitting the pavement and shutting off the rest of the world. But for me, it can be hard to shut off the brain. It becomes an internal scrolling ticker, which might take me anywhere, from work thoughts to remembrances of my grandmother to a sudden mournful recollection of my great friend and mentor back at the *Palm Beach Post*, also a runner, Chris Stanke. *I feel terrible ... I can't lift my feet ... how am I going to run three miles feeling like this? ... OK, OK, you always feel this way during the first half-mile or so, just suck it up ... Breathe deep, relax your shoulders, shift your hips slightly forward so you don't kill your back ... "I know I was born and I know that I'll die, the in between is mine, I am mine." ... I love Eddie Vedder ... Damn it, I forgot to write out my budget for tomorrow's Olympics coverage. Mental reminder to get that done ... "One mile completed. Time, 11 minutes, 54 seconds. Average pace, 11:58 per mile." ... Going too slow, but can't pick it up just yet. I'll wait until I am halfway there. ... OH-OH, Living on a prayer! ... Stop it, focus. ... I am leaning forward too much. Hips. Shoulders. Breathe. OK, you can do this. ... I have to call her when I get home. I forgot to call yesterday and I have to see how her doctor's appointment went. I really hope she doesn't bring up the Obama thing again ... "Halfway point, 1-point-5-zero miles to go. Time, fifteen minutes, twenty-three seconds. Average pace, 11:50 per mile." Yes! My pace is lower. OK, feeling better now. ... The sun feels good. ... Joanne, are you up there somewhere? ... My grandma might have liked running ... Stanke, this one is for you, buddy.*

Doesn't everyone have this internal monologue raging as they run?

★ ★ ★ ★ ★

"I'm sorry."

After my first night run, I sat in my car and tried to absorb what had just happened. I was appreciating this for what it was – a run in its best, purest form. I normally would rely on music to push me through the last mile. This time, I took in the elements rather than fight them. Outside the bouncing beam of my headlamp and a trickle of light from a random house or two, it was just me, in the dark, on a quiet, forested block in a neighborhood my friends sarcastically refer to as the sticks.

My senses were overloaded again as soon as I walked through the front door. I petted the puppy, kissed my husband, grabbed a water and then called my mother.

"Guess what I just did?" I blurted out.

"Does this have to do with the dog?" she asked.

"No! I went for my first night run!" I said.

"What? In that weath-thah?"

"Mom, it wasn't bad out at all. No wind. But I had to do at least a few miles because of the race."

"Oh, that's right. I'm coming up for that, God willing."

Life had caught up to my mother again. In a year's span, she'd developed major groin pain, and after way too many tests and way too little insight from a gaggle of inept physicians, the diagnosis was two pinched nerves and bone spurs in her back. I went down to Florida to be with her and my father for the surgery. No matter how routine the procedure, nothing prepares you for seeing your parent coming out of surgery, pale from anesthesia, begging for something to make the pain and nausea stop. Nothing prepares you for the reality that your time with your parents is finite. I cried that night, alone, thinking of what was to come for my mother, but also crying as it sunk in how much time I'd wasted. I'd had enough of arguing with my mother and trying to prove I was right. I'd had enough of trying so hard to avoid comparing myself to her, as if it was this awful, terrible thing. By letting all that go, all in a rush, I was finally able to accept a part of myself that lay dormant and hidden for far too long.

I saw a person who was flawed, but a person who had fight. I saw a person who loved and cared for her family, even if the way she loved and cared wasn't always what I thought I needed. I saw a person who didn't have a chance to accomplish or aim for things I mostly took for granted, and while she may have had regrets, she'd always been strong in her support of me. By seeing all of that, I was able to have my Aurora moment, even if it came without the "Fan-fucking-tastic" part. (I'm still working on that, by the way.)

"God willing?" I asked her. "What is the latest development?"

"I'll get a second opinion, but I may have to have another surgery," she said.

"Look Mom, don't get too far ahead of yourself," I told her. "Try to keep your spirits up, and don't forget to turn off the brain every once in a while."

She had to laugh at that.

"OK, well, be careful when you go out there," she said. "And take care of yourself. Love you," she added, closing with her consistent signoff.

"I will. Love you, too."

And the next run will be for you, Mom.

ANNE MILLIGAN, an employment lawyer in Portland, Oregon, has represented clients in eight federal districts and before the Bureau of Labor and Industries. She is a former writer and content manager for *Run Oregon*.

3

CHASING SHADOWS THROUGH THE NIGHT

BY ANNE MILLIGAN

Little Rock, Arkansas

I had decided to kill myself. It was early winter and the Great Recession had slouched into its darkest corner. On the rotting floor of my hundred-year-old rental, eleven months of rejection letters slowly yellowed. I checked the tally I kept beside my Compaq Presario, an aging laptop with six keys missing and a battery that never held more than sixty seconds of charge. A form rejection email in the morning and a crisp, white "no" received by first-class mail that afternoon had brought the total to 356.

What I felt was not quite sadness, nor was it depression. Every languid, enervated day was a fever dream from which there was no hope of waking. I hadn't always been hopeless, but hard times carve out either a new depth of character or a void in its place. I stared at the pile of rejection letters and smoothed my hands down the long black apron I wore over a tight, black shirt and slacks. Bits of brown rice and Kung Pao sauce clung to the fabric. I sighed and scratched at the orange stain with the worn-down nail of my index finger. I couldn't stop thinking about what one of my regulars at the small dim sum restaurant where I worked had asked me that evening.

"You seem like such a smart girl," she'd said with distressing urgency. "Are you ever going to do something with your life?"

Her words hit me with the force of a back-handed slap across my face. I was speechless. Do something? I couldn't tell her that I was actually an attorney who had graduated tenth in her class. Unfortunately for me and thousands of other new lawyers chin-deep in debt, the American Bar Association called the class of 2010 "The Lost Year," and projected that half of us would never practice the law a single day in our lives. I could tell from the way this customer spoke to me that she assumed I was a single mother in a dead-end job. She hoped that her question might reawaken long dormant academic aspirations in me. Instead, all that surfaced was bitter disappointment.

Now it was late: 10:30 p.m. in the twenty-fourth most dangerous city in the United States. I stripped the food-smudged clothes from my body and slipped into a skintight pair of hand-me-down shorts with a faded "IN SPORT" logo on the left leg. I pulled on one, two, three, four Target sports bras and a red singlet I'd gotten on clearance, one of only two athletic shirts I owned. I tied a house key onto my shoelaces and burst out into the night, south on Rice, west on Third, north on Thayer, west on Markham, climbing up Kavanaugh Hill. It was the same dark, four-mile out-and-back almost every night, on a stretch of roads known for armed robberies and brazen, daytime burglaries. I'd just started running that year and should have been more attuned to the dangers of my route; instead, I felt indifferent. Fear is a scarce commodity when you're no longer committed to being alive.

Breathe, step-step. Breathe, step-step. No music – the only rhythm of my run was legs and lungs. Breathe, step-step. "How would I do it?" I wondered. I didn't own a gun or any pills, and there weren't many tall places in town from which to leap. The selfishness of the gas stove approach was staggering, and in any case we didn't have one. I wondered how serious I was about this decision, as though I was outside of myself, as though the choice would be made with or without me. Breathe, step-step. Breathe, step-step.

I struck a bargain with myself. If I didn't have a job by the end of March – a safe five months in the future – I would Virginia Woolf myself into the Arkansas River. Most women who commit suicide want to leave a beautiful corpse, but I wanted to dissolve and decay into the water, for my soft skin to be torn apart by the underwater brush and powerful currents of a Mississippi River tributary. I hoped that my remains would never be found and that eventually, the humiliation and failure I'd left behind would be forgotten.

After I'd made my choice and set a deadline, a great comfort settled around me like a warm fog. I shared my secret with no one. I wanted no one's pity, derision or –

worst of all – their aphoristic empathy. I just wanted to be done, one way or another, whatever it took. I continued to work and run alone at night, letting the days slip by me in a cold blur.

★ ★ ★ ★ ★

PORTLAND, OREGON

On the last day of my junior year of high school, I ran out the front door of my parents' home and never looked back. To return the favor, my mother immediately drained the entire balance of $2,000 from my checking account, which she'd had to co-sign on. I was seventeen years old and alone in the world, penniless despite having worked so hard to save that $2,000. Looking back, the day I ran away was the first time I'd ever really *run* – I'd always refused to give the fitness tests in school any effort, walking the slowest mile imaginable in pointless teenage protest. A woman I barely knew took me in and let me live with her until I could afford rent in another family's basement, in the school district where I'd finish my senior year.

Flash forward a decade, and Katie – my savior at seventeen – had come through for me again. I stepped off the plane into a cold, gray February in Portland, twenty-two hundred miles from the place I'd called home for the last ten years. It was the first time I'd ever been to the West Coast, and I was slated to stay with Katie's half-sister's elderly aunt, Trudi, Trudi's partner of three decades, and an assortment of aging cats. Objectively, I knew that what I was doing didn't make any sense. Here

I was in Portland, sitting for the Oregon Bar Exam and running my second half marathon, simultaneously planning my future and my death. It was a robotic sort of dedication that I'd learned in minimum wage jobs and mastered in law school, pushing forward on all fronts until the day, whenever it came, that the axe finally fell.

Strangely (or perhaps not) I was more nervous about my race than I was about sitting for the bar exam. Talk of an ice storm circulated in the news, and it had been nearly six months since I'd run in the sunlight. Would the ice make a difference? Would the sun? I'd been in the dark so long, I didn't know if I needed sunglasses, a hat — did *anyone* wear sunscreen in Portland, moreover in February? What if running during the day was something completely different than running at night? A small part of me wondered if I would find out something awful about running or myself the next day, as I had in Montreal six months before. In Quebec, the sour lessons I learned left me dry-heaving through the last four miles of my first road race, stumbling towards the mirage of the Stade Olympique.

Portland was my last chance to redeem myself from that fiasco. Early the next morning, I tottered off the light-rail train and greeted the frigid race day in a trash bag. At that hour near the 45th parallel it was hard to tell whether the sun had come, was coming, or had given up on the city all together. I took in the small scene around me in abated shock. In Montreal, I'd raced with over twenty-one thousand runners from thirty countries from the Pont Jacques-Cartier through rose-strewn, raucous streets marked in kilometers. Downtown Portland, in contrast, greeted me with a thousand shivering runners, at least a third of whom seemed to be openly sneering at my strange fashion choice.

Before I could even consider whether I cared, the gun went off. Learning from old mistakes, I carried my own water, refused all Gu, and wore good shoes. Most importantly of all, I hadn't attempted to fit three long runs into the week before the race. After a flat 5K, I pushed up the long Terwilliger Boulevard climb, slow and steady, letting the hill come to my feet. Breathe, step-step, breathe. In the distance I saw a pin turn in the road ahead, a glimmer of hope that the downhill was just around that bend – only to see another hill. Another corner: another climb. Corner and climb, corner and climb, again and again. I was furious and near tears. What did you expect? I yelled silently. It's called the Heartbreaker Half for a reason. Buckle down: barricade your heart. You'll make it, but it won't be beautiful.

I faced the asphalt and pushed upward until a panicked heat flushed over my body. That was it. I couldn't do this anymore. I looked up for the first time in miles, hoping to locate a golf cart that would carry me back downtown; instead, I saw the crest of the hill and felt a smile erupt across my face. While runners around me gingerly trotted down the hill, I was a new woman, ready to start a brand new race. I stretched out my legs into a wide sprint, and barreled down the hill, so hot I thought my feet would dissolve underneath me. I pulled ahead of dozens of racers, running faster than I'd ever run in my life, running without any of the walk breaks that were a staple of my training. I crossed the finish line a champion in my own mind, and promptly collapsed onto the sidewalk.

★ ★ ★ ★ ★

LITTLE ROCK, ARKANSAS

"So I see from your résumé that you haven't done anything since you graduated from law school. Ten months, just sitting at home. Why is that?" The middle-aged man before me leaned dangerously back in his leather office chair, his face now out of range of the low, ambient light. I felt all the blood in my body rush to the skin of my cheeks.

"That isn't true. I've been waiting tables since the day after the bar exam. I just didn't put that on there – I – I didn't think it was relevant to legal employment," I stumbled.

"Oh. Good. I just thought you were lazy, perhaps."

This exchange left me dazed through the next several questions. I came back to my senses sometime around the moment he asked me to divide 278 by twelve without a calculator.

"May I have a piece of paper?" I asked. He pushed a sheet across to me, and I scribbled multiplication tables vigorously, trying to find the answer in reverse. I pushed my answer back – the man shrugged despite the fact that I was confident that I was right.

"What year was the Magna Carta signed?" I blinked profusely – history had never been my forte.

"15…12?" I asked, trying to obscure my horror at the man's increasingly difficult and irrelevant questions.

"Hmm," he replied with a flawless poker face, scrawling illegible notes on a yellow legal pad.[1]

I was back in Arkansas, but the fever that came over

---

[1] The Magna Carta was actually signed in 1215.

me in the Pacific Northwest was still with me. I had made a bargain with myself that March would be the last month that I would suffer through unemployment, bitter cold, a decaying home and soul-crushing debt. It was now March 22. There were nine days left in the month. And I was in the middle of an interview from hell for a job I wasn't convinced I wanted.

"When was the last time you lied, and what did you lie about?"

I sighed. "I don't know. Maybe last week? It was probably food-related."

"What do you mean," he frowned.

"Like, 'No, I didn't eat the other cookie,' but I actually did? That kind of thing?"

I wondered if my voice had squeaked, wondered if he was buying any of this. I imagined myself as calm as Madam President, but my heart raced in my chest and I thought I would choke at any moment. I glanced furtively at my empty water glass and resigned myself: I wasn't getting this job. The Magna Carta answer alone had to have blown my chances. This was it.

"When was the last time you got drunk?"

"My birthday," I said. "March 10. I turned twenty-seven."

"Congratulations," he smirked, scrawling more characters on his pad. "Name every drug you've ever taken, the frequency of your usage, and the last time you took each drug."

Letting go – something distance running had taught me, a trait that had never come naturally – released me from hope. I felt emancipated from myself and all my expectations. I answered his question completely and honestly, with dates, names and explanations. The man sat forward in his chair.

"What does that drug do?"

"Supposedly a sense of euphoria, but I didn't experience that. Just wasn't able to sleep very well. It may not have been real. It may have been something else, or nothing. I'll never know."

Nine days. Just nine days left in the month. This stark fact suddenly tainted my disassociation from the unearthly interview and made the delirium in me ache. The man switched his line of questioning to a more traditional vein and, having been unemployed so long, I had a reserve of prepared answers to recite.

"Well, I have to say, Ms. Milligan, I am very impressed."

I struggled not to look shocked. "Thank you, sir."

"You seem like a very hard worker, dedicated, sharp and extremely calm under pressure. I like that. I'd like to offer you a job here at the firm."

I stared at him in complete disbelief. Was this real life? Was he still prying at my psyche, ready to give and take away merely to gauge and categorize my reaction? Nine days. The words echoed in my head.

"Perhaps you need some time to think about it," he asked. "A husband or fiancé you want to talk it over with?"

The sexism of his question stung me. The importance of this choice was so much greater than he could ever imagine. I was to take the job and live, or reject it and let go of life – that was my choice alone. I smiled, stood, and extended my hand.

"Thank you very much. Yes. I'll let you know tomorrow morning at the latest."

The man shook my hand so hard I thought he would break it. I still felt the impression of his skin as I walked out of the building into a dimming asphalt lot. Nine days; a setting sun; a morning deadline – it was time to run.

* * * * *

Washington, D.C.

I woke up alone in a pitch black room at the Omni Shoreham, an opulent but aging four-diamond hotel that in its past life hosted inaugural balls for every president from Roosevelt to Clinton. It was the weekend after the first Monday in October, when the Supreme Court of the United States reconvenes to hear cases after summer recess. The firm had sent me to D.C. on business, but my elation over being just three miles from the National Mall had kept me awake for most the night.

I slipped out of bed and peered out the window over a black forest. The Washington Monument peeked over the edge of the trees in the distance, an illuminated exclamation point shooting out into the night: Something bright in the center of me came to attention. I knew I had to run to it right then and there. I pulled on my shoes, strapped on my phone, and tiptoed to the gilded elevator. As the golden doors closed, I stared at my own reflection. How would I get there? I'd been in D.C. for a grand total of twelve hours. I was mapless and inexperienced.

Go south, I thought. Your body will take you where you need to be. I slipped past the concierge like a prisoner, afraid for some reason that he would judge me for being up so early with no idea where I would be in an hour's time. I wondered if he knew that I was actually still secretly poor; I wondered if he knew I didn't belong. Out into the acreage, out into the black I went. At ground level, the lights of the Mall were nowhere to be seen and I was soon in the same kind of forest that fairy tales warn children about.

As I ran over a stone bridge, I could make out a cemetery so old it couldn't have interned a body since fire destroyed Constantinople. I breathed in the fog that rolled over the old headstones and tried to stay calm, despite the youthful superstitions that rose in me at the sight of that old earth. I had run a mile, two miles – an eternity – but the sky was still so dark and the ground so foreign: I was terrified, listening for every crackling autumn leaf, any sign that I was poised to be ejected from the woods.

I ran with my torso straight as a board and breathed proudly; at a minimum, no one would know how scared I was. Maybe that false confidence alone would get me through the trees. Suddenly as I ran, it struck me that I had felt this way before. This deep, aching fear was no different than what I'd felt for three years in law school. I spent every day there convinced I had no allies, that I would be found out as a fake, that my minimal intelligence, failed beauty, and waves of emotional incapacity would root me out for what I was: nothing. To the world, I was confident and implacable. With time, though, they would discover my flaws and push me aside. Sure enough, when I graduated from law school all my fears were realized. No one wanted me. It was just as I'd suspected all those years. I didn't belong, and almost died for it.

Though the strongest stars still shone, I began to see them recede into the navy above as I continued to run, my heart empty. The trees had given way to urban streets and offices, street lamps and traffic circles, but the city still slept. She was mine for the moment, and I would not share her with anyone else.

"Three point five miles," my phone mechanically announced, jarring me out of a meditative stupor. Where was I? Two guards walked slowly through the night around a monstrous, white acropolis, batons in hand, the cadence of their steps so patient and grim. I came to a walk as I peered around the corner, coming upon a litany of steps. Five young men, perhaps no more than seventeen years old, sat on the second-to-last step, watching the edges of the horizon grow brighter over a long, shallow pool. Without warning, I saw him: Abraham Lincoln, seated nineteen feet tall in Georgia white marble.

I was already out of breath from the run, but the sight took even more air from my lungs: the Lincoln Memorial, deserted but for one photographer and a handful of teenage boys watching the sunrise in the wrong direction. Less than two miles from here the man had been shot to death, and for the life of me I could not remember if this was merely a colossal monument or his grave. I passed through the huge columns and approached this man's temple gingerly in case his tomb was in fact somewhere beneath the soles of my shoes. He'd been a lawyer and an outsider, too. Depression haunted him his entire life; but what greatness he had achieved.

Time didn't stop; it became irrelevant. I stayed staring at Mr. Lincoln until my heart stilled and the moment became electric. I had so much farther to go. I knew so little of history, but it was still two miles to the Capitol steps and, I hoped, many decades to go before I left what I had come to realize was a very short life.

I ran and ran, through the newly minted Martin Luther King, Jr. Memorial opened less than two months before, crisp, fluorescent white and staring out from a *Star Wars*-style carbonite, past the memorials for the great wars, across the Tidal Basin to a circular colonnade of columns covered by a shallow dome. As I stepped into the open air memorial I read the words of the Declaration of Independence engraved into the walls to the left of a great bronze man. I'd left the Mall without even knowing it, chasing shadows through the last moments of the night. I lay down on the cold stone floor and stared up at a weak sun creaking through the dome above.

PETE DANKO reports on renewable energy and local business in Portland, Oregon, and is a wine-industry marketing and public relations consultant. His work has appeared in publications including the *San Francisco Chronicle* and the *New York Times.*

4

OFF THE TRAIL WITH
FORTY-SEVEN MILES TO GO

BY PETE DANKO

I was working hard not to be alone. From time to time I'd see the headlamp or flashlight of a fellow runner or the vague illumination of ground or brush or trees, and I'd pick up my pace to stay connected to the light. I didn't want to be on my own out here, God knows where. I needed a guide, if only for confirmation that I hadn't gone wildly off track. This seemed especially important three and a half miles into a fifty-mile race, but it wasn't my only concern. The same desire to avoid disaster early – to keep this from becoming the fiasco it had every right to be – had me stepping gingerly to avoid the rocks or roots that surely lay in wait, eager to fling me to the ground in a bloodied, broken heap or even worse, send me tumbling down a bluff toward the river. Wasn't there a river lurking out there somewhere?

The realization that we would run in darkness had come to me, abruptly, an hour or so earlier as I joined a scattering of shivering, chattering runners drifting toward the start of the Autumn Leaves 50. I had factored a predawn start into my prerace contemplations, but with the thought that it would be, I don't know, *kind of* dark, and not for very long. With the race set to begin at 6 a.m., I had even wondered if my LED headlamp would be necessary. But away from the campfire, where we had been warming ourselves, it was indeed very dark – still. This first Saturday in November, it turned out, was also the last day of daylight savings time. Of the three hundred and sixty-five days of the year, this was the one when the sun would arrive latest, at 7:53 a.m. here just north of the 45th parallel.

"They say the darkest hour is right before the dawn," the great man once warbled, a truth I knew well from getting up countless times in the small hours and driving empty highways and roads for weekend races that began at 7 or 8 a.m. These solo drives came to be integral aspects of the race experience, adventures of their own, the mind one moment undertaking a furious review of key items that might have been left behind, the next stressing about some aspect of the course, or an injury, or a goal, only to be rescued by the distraction of middle-of-the-night, over-the-air radio: the BBC World Service, or strange snippets of talk at the far end of the AM dial. One drive to an especially early and stress-inducing race brought a diversion that will never be topped – a long, earnest interview with a man who had been a horse. You laugh, but for me it was a lifesaver. Right up to when the horn sounded that blustery morning in Coeur d'Alene, Idaho, sending me and 2,400 other wetsuit-clad swimmers into the washing machine that is the Ironman swim, whenever panic began to encroach I thought about Horse Man, and chuckled, and for a moment my anxiety was eased.

Autumn Leaves was different; I drove out to the site in a state of unusual calm. I had never run past 26.2 miles, and in the previous six months my longest outing, in training or otherwise, was 13.1 miles – true. But those same daunting facts made Autumn Leaves less worrying. They convinced me that it wasn't a race, it was a lark, a wonderfully foolish venture. For the first time in memory, having a successful day wouldn't be a matter of how long it took me to get to the finish line. All I had to do was make it all the way. I like notching new personal records – hell, let's be honest: I worship at the altar of the PR – but going for it every race can wear on you, physically and mentally, even if no one else in the entire world cares how fast you are (or aren't). There was a part of me that had grown envious of those runners who could proclaim victory merely by finishing. Now I had found a race where that would be the case for me, although this matter of the darkness, well, that did begin to put a different spin on things.

★ ★ ★ ★ ★

The gun sounded and our clump of maybe a hundred runners advanced up the roadway. We all knew there was a very long way to go, so we proceeded with little of the shuffling and darting that reorders a nervous field in shorter races. Also, I was not eager to find clear space – another departure from the norm. I don't know how anyone else felt, but I was glad to be among other runners. The extent of my headlamp's individual contribution could not be deciphered, lost in a collection of lights that projected the scene in the way of an early-days film, almost strobe-lit, a jittery picture but one complete enough to show the way, and illuminating enough to reveal the impressive diversity of the ultra crowd.

We ranged from twenty-somethings to graybeards. With the temperature hovering around freezing, most everyone was bundled from head to toe, but here and there I spotted men – no women – with bare limbs, like me. In shorter races, my pace would often leave me in a forest of skinny legs, feeling self-conscious about my thick thighs and calves, the odd oak among aspens. Here, in the new world of the ultra, in the strange light, I was happy to note an assortment of shapes and sizes.

After a few minutes shuffling along on a road, essentially warming up, we weaved through what seemed to be a parking lot and then onto paved path, carefully negotiating surface changes. It was 6:05 a.m. and it was dark but my senses were electric, gauging every footfall with precision over clean roadway, gravel-strewn pavement, an interval of dirt, a moss-covered curb.

Faster runners pulled away and slower ones settled behind and there I was as we moved along, in a loose amalgam of middle-of-the-packers. A few yards separated those of us in this itinerant crew. I peered up ahead at the diminishing signs of the leaders and was grateful for my middling talent. What a burden it would be to be the one up front, leading the charge into the black!

With less in the way of group light now, to see the ground in front of me I adjusted the tilt of my headlamp slightly upward, compensating for the fact that I naturally run looking down (a style that has produced many an unattractive race photo). There was so much curiosity running through my mind and, blissfully, none of it involved how I might actually manage to run fifty miles. Calm as I was about this undertaking before the race, I had expected it would begin to work on me once we got going. That's just the way it goes in long races. Short ones, too. We've all been there – no matter how much we love running, no matter how much we hunger to push ourselves beyond our limits. To race is to look forward to the finish. After a mile in a marathon, we tell ourselves: "That wasn't difficult. Just do it twenty-five more times. Miles are easy. Just keep doing them." This does not have the intended effect. *Twenty-five more?* The undertaking only becomes more daunting. And as we near ten miles we imagine being buoyed by breaking into double figures – only to realize that nothing has really changed, still we must battle onward, hopeful that the halfway point will be the magic switch that makes the going easier.

Instead, I was finding, the challenge and excitement of running in darkness became a shield – for now – protecting me from the constant cogitating about distance done and distance to go. The mystery of the darkness was more alluring – and the fact that I had moved to Portland just four months earlier heightened the sensation. To put it bluntly, I had no idea where I was running. In my mind, this place, Champoeg State Park, was little more than a green splotch on a map about twenty-five miles southwest of Portland, hugging the Willamette as the river made several sharp bends in picking its slow way through the valley to meet the Columbia. We had been given some information on the course, but it was scant: We'd run a flat loop, just shy of five miles in length, some combination of bike path and dirt trail, ten times, with a beginning 1.2-mile out-and-back on a service road to round out the distance.

Off that service road and onto the bike path, it was pitch dark as we hit another patch of fog. And weren't we running through the black of the nighttime forest, through stands of Douglas fir? Uncertainty reigned, but these were my suppositions. The campfire had been surrounded by trees. I had noted glimpses of trees early in the run, when we runners were together and could jointly muster the candlepower to light our immediate surroundings. Now, who knew? I lifted and turned my head to try to get a better sense of things, but there was no telling. My light barely made it to the ground now, where it showed bare, damp asphalt and an occasional leaf. Pointed higher, the beam died in frozen fog, revealing nothing. We seemed in some great void, running through space. Fear began to creep into my consciousness, and I tried to fight it off by recalling the primal wonder and mystery of night running that I had known before and that I hoped with each step to reconnect with.

★ ★ ★ ★ ★

My first sustained experiences with night running came when I was a young sportswriter living in Riverside, California. My sport of choice then was mountain biking, but I would throw in a five-mile run or two each week for variety's sake. In blazing, inland Southern California, for all but a few months of the year the options were to run very early or very late in the day. I could and would get up at dawn for a bike ride, but then as now the runner wanted to go later, after the muscles and joints were loose and after some good work had been accomplished.

Night, I soon found, brought new dimensions to running. Speed, for instance. Science insists we don't actually go faster at night. Science says we fall prey to a trick of perception, that because we can only see what's nearer, and what's nearer comes and goes more quickly than what's distant, we *think* we're moving faster. I don't doubt this science, as far as it goes; but when it comes to running I've learned that the only experiments that matter are the ones we conduct on ourselves. Do I — or, more accurately — *can I* run faster at night? I put this proposition to the test not long ago.

It was January and I was a month into making my way back from a foot injury and a bit of a holiday break. My plan one Sunday was to run five or six easy miles, but the day got away from me and by late afternoon I found myself planted in front of the television watching the San Francisco 49ers play the New York Giants with the Super Bowl on the line. This was the rare football game that might hold my interest, with outlines of great sports drama evident from the start, but in the second quarter I was struggling to maintain my concentration. I wanted to run.

It was a typical damp, cloud-shrouded day in Portland, and the meager dull light of midwinter afternoon was leaking away as sunset neared. Would I run? I wasn't completely sold on the idea, but during that interminable manufactured intermission the NFL calls the two-minute warning I put on my shorts, two or three thin layers of shirts and my shoes.

I fired up the Garmin and set it outside so it could find its satellites. Would I run? I still wasn't completely convinced. It was dark now. And chilly. The glowing television, like a warm fireplace, had a pretty good grip on me. Then the 49ers ran out the clock to end the half. Without really thinking about it I got up, went out the door, strapped on the Garmin, hit go and went – into the night.

Twenty minutes and twenty-two seconds. That's how long it took me to run 5K with no warm-up and no competition to egg me on, along an ad hoc, twisting and turning course through my North Tabor neighborhood's narrow wet streets, dark save for the occasional glistening of street lamp or the light from an approaching automobile. I'm barely a sub-nineteen-minute 5K man in my very best condition, running tucked behind a faster dude to pull me along. This halftime dash was a good two minutes quicker than I should have been able to run. How to explain it? Simple: The thrill of speeding through the night made me faster. It often had in Riverside, too, twenty years earlier, where on a wide boulevard near our apartment lined with impossibly tall, thin palms, palms that reached hundreds of feet into the air, their shining tops swaying in the moonlight like dancers, I would race by, buoyant, flying.

★ ★ ★ ★ ★

Was there a moon at Autumn Leaves? Just the tiniest sliver of one, the historical tables reveal. I don't recall seeing it. A big, fluorescent, full one sure would have come in handy. We left the bike path and were now on dirt. I could see nothing beyond what was in the small circle of light provided by my headlamp, but after a hundred yards or so – still dirt – I surmised that this was not a brief interlude of trail; we had entered the mile and a half single-track portion of the circuit. I was terrified.

Veteran ultra runners – those who have knocked off plenty of 100-milers, not the half-assed 50s I've done – will laugh.

A mile and a half of nighttime trail? Try twenty, thirty miles of trail in the dark, buddy – and try it after you've run sixty or seventy miles. Then you'll know something about the tricks the mind can play in the deep weird darkness of the nighttime trail. Then branches will become snakes. Rocks or trees up ahead will appear as skunks or mountain lions or old girlfriends. Then a long period of silence – or what feels like a long period of silence, who knows how long it's really been, for nothing you see or hear or smell now can be trusted – will get you thinking: "That sign told me to go left at that last fork, right? But aren't we supposed to be along the creek? Where's the creek? I don't hear a creek!"

My first reaction was to ratchet up my already intense efforts to keep others – their lights, at least – in sight. But this was proving difficult and confusing. Lights came and went. Lights were simultaneously way off to the right, or straight ahead, or off to the left. What the hell? Well of course: The trail wound around, circled, dipped, rose, cut in and out of the trees (or so I assumed). I risked speeding up to get closer to whoever was in front of me. It was easy. I was fresh, and I had night's performance-enhancing effect on my side.

I was relieved to reach a guy. "Hey," I said with manufactured casualness as he looked back toward me. With apparent disinterest, he grunted an unknown syllable in reply. We ran on, me behind him, now feeling safe enough to allow my thoughts to wander, if briefly, to consideration of the chunky form that flashed before me. Was it his first ultra – and as much a lark as mine? I had to ask. "Uh, no, no, I've done quite a few," he allowed, each word arriving slowly, interrupted by two or three well-chosen steps. This information, though a bit surprising, fit with what I had come to gather about ultra runners at the race start – that they aren't all 3 percent body fat freaks. Where earlier this had been comforting information, now it began to deflate the challenge I was undertaking. *Fat people can do this,* I sighed. *No, no!* came the internal retort: The *thick-hewn* thrive going long.

My contemplation was abruptly interrupted.

Chunky Guy had stopped.

"This isn't right," he said.

I pulled in behind him.

"Yeah, we were supposed to go left back there. Yeah, this creek is wrong." He smirked. Assessing this smirk, there, in the mostly dark, barely into a fifty-mile run, I was reassured. Yes, it was the smirk of a man who knew precisely where he had gone wrong.

"So, you know where we are?"

"Yeah," he said.

Chunky led us back a bit, maybe for a minute, and damned if there wasn't a runner right there, peeling left where we had peeled right. We followed, letting a little more slack into the string that tied us together. I was third in the line of three – and hadn't noticed a light behind me – but was still tethered, which is all that really mattered when my right toe found a tree root, sending me diving into the dirt.

If anything was badly damaged, I didn't feel it as adrenaline shot through me. There was no danger I was anything more than scraped up, but there was the terrifying risk of being left behind – or spotted down, scrambling for the headlamp that, headless, lay a few feet in front of me, its light directed upward in a shaft that could have been fog or might have been dust I'd provoked. In no time, I was up and moving along, a comfortable ten yards behind my couriers.

* * * * *

I had a plan to walk a portion of each loop. This was a preservation strategy adopted from the marathon guru Jeff Galloway. He advises that runners can end up completing the marathon faster if they incorporate periodic walk intervals – say, thirty seconds of walking for each five minutes of running for faster runners, or a minute of walking for each twelve or thirteen minutes of running for slower runners. I'd never heard of a faster runner using this scheme. I, in fast-hole fashion (you don't really need to be fast to be a fast-hole), thought of it as a way for not-fit-enough people to go farther than they really ought to. And that is why it came to mind for me as Autumn Leaves approached.

During the first three miles of the race, the walking idea was buried under the excitement of being off on a fifty-mile adventure and doing so in the dark. Then, having been lost (and found) and fallen (and gotten up) – so Biblical! – and apparently drained of my adrenaline stores, I remembered: Oh, yeah, I'm supposed to walk. It was the wise thing to do. The sane thing to do. The only thing to do.

But I resisted. Yes, partly for the reason so many people resist: It was early in the race and I wasn't tired – why the hell would I walk? But of course the very point of the strategy is to force oneself to minimize energy expenditure early in the race in order to avoid the grim but common death-march scenario. I lectured myself on these truths, but kept running up against the real reason I could not now walk: No friggin' way I was going to walk and let my guides up ahead leave me behind! I kept them near as we wound along a wiggly, slightly undulating path. Post-fall, I was more fixated on the ground, alert to roots and rocks, but mostly what I saw were leaves. Autumn Leaves, indeed.

We arrived back safely where we had begun, our first of ten loops completed. I can report that during Loop 2, the world around me began to lighten. Day was not breaking, but night knew what was coming and, in some just-perceptible way, was preparing for the inevitable. This unfolding of a new day is something we have all experienced, I suppose, whether we've woken up before the alarm went off and sat in the breakfast nook with a cup of coffee in deep contemplation as the backyard accepts the first rays of the day; or if we have stirred early and perched on a promenade at Yosemite as light creeps over and transforms one of those big, famous rocks. Sunrise is always glorious and beautiful, so predictably glorious and beautiful that it is a great wonder of life and a pity that we all don't get up every day for it.

This wasn't a sunrise, per se, at least not yet, but I submit that it was even better. Never was a man more primed for it than I was then. The first loop had given me a measure of confidence that I could make my way around the course and had heightened the sense of mystery of what was out there. So on Loop 2, I spent less time enslaved by the spot of ground my headlamp showed. I unchained myself – not just my eyes, but all of my senses, and my mind – to engage my surroundings.

I could begin to see the vague silhouettes of trees, sometimes shrouded in fog, sometimes not. I heard, just barely, a car on a roadway distant, surely outside the park. When it faded away, the sounds were of my footsteps, crunching along on the leaves, and my breathing, not yet labored. I considered my pace: still too fast, still pulled along by the forces of the night, even as they receded, but certainly less fevered than before.

Onward, I noticed there were places where the terrain opened up, prairie-like. On Loop 3, the strange little trees I thought I had seen dotting this plain were revealed to be made of metal – they were the "holes" for the Champoeg disc golf course. The river revealed itself not long after that, through mostly naked alders and ash, down a sharp, berry-bramble shrouded bank that – still assessing the threat risk – I figured would have stopped a wayward runner before he hit water some thirty feet below. It was the same Willamette I had swum in two month earlier, in the City of Portland Triathlon, right downtown, where the river, even when it is down, moves with some energy and bounce. Here: so flat, so quiet, as to seem stopped.

Finally, somewhere on that third loop, I found myself running under a canopy still holding autumn foliage, a tunnel of sorts, now lit softly from within, somehow, all golden and strangely bright. I pulled off my headlamp and put it in my fanny pack. I slowed to a walk. There was no reason not to. There was nothing to be afraid of anymore. Night was gone. There was a feeling of an ending, and of a beginning. Thirty-five miles to go.

The nomadic **VANESSA RUNS**, who roams the land in an RV, is a self-described "author, trail nerd, elevation junkie and mountain-loving dirtbag." Her books include *Daughters of Distance* and *The Summit Seeker*.

5

THE LAND OF THE MIDNIGHT SUN

BY VANESSA RUNS

I have a dream of someday running the full length of the Alaska Highway, which winds from British Columbia, through the Yukon, and finally into Alaska, a challenge more commonly tackled by bikers or cyclists. The highway is the most beautiful I have ever seen, with a side of danger that gives me goose bumps. Moose outnumber people two to one in the Yukon. Traffic jams are caused by wildlife, not cars. Close to 80 percent of the territory remains pristine wilderness.

Alaska is home to thirty-thousand grizzlies, more than twenty times the number in the Lower 48. Scary as that sounds, I'm told a moose attack is statistically more likely – but in Haines, Alaska, I fed a moose a banana and kissed her on the nose. So there. Bear, moose, sheep and bison sightings are frequent on the highway. In a span of two hours of driving, we managed to see: fifty bison, twenty-five sheep, two moose, a caribou and a bear. Humans are out of place here, awkwardly weaving an asphalt path through the forest.

Yes, I want to run the highway, all 1,387 miles of it. Running the highway would guarantee face-to-face wildlife encounters, just the sort of adrenaline-fired jolt I look for in running. Some people run to lose weight, or to cross achievements off a list, or to clear their mind – and those are all worthy motivations. For me it is fear that drives me to run. Night running is the only activity I do where I can consistently take on and overcome my fears. It doesn't matter how long I've been running or how experienced I've become, there will always be something new to scare me. I might be startled by an unexpected meeting with a wild animal or unnerved by a steep and rocky descent. Running at night invites the crazy, someday notion of running the Alaska Highway.

* * * * *

In *At Day's Close: Night in Times Past*, Roger Ekirch laments that nighttime has become the forgotten half of human experience. There used to be a time when the cover of darkness liberated people. Social conventions took a backseat to primal impulses and the unapologetic pursuit of pleasure. Through running, I know that freedom. At night, I am no longer a trespasser picking my way through the trail. I become part of its ecosystem, just another animal in the wild. Sharpened senses and enlarged pupils guide my path. Hunting down my competition, I am a force to be reckoned with. Although these moments of euphoria are worth the physical exertion, the lows can also feel overwhelming.

It wasn't anything as exotic as the Yukon or Alaska and there were no grizzlies to fear (or moose to feed), but on my thirty-first birthday, I decided to try a nighttime running experience with a different twist. I set off to do a self-supported birthday run on the beautiful Wildwood Trail in Forest Park in Portland, Oregon. The tradition among ultramarathon trail runners is to run one mile for every year on your birthday – thirty-one miles for me. Instead, I opted for the lofty goal of running one hour for every year, a whopping thirty-one hours of nonstop running. I had borrowed the idea from Catra Corbett, the tattooed ultrarunning superstar mentioned in Christopher McDougall's famous book, *Born to Run*. At the Ridgecrest 50K in California, Catra helped me through a slump by passing me, then calling for me to follow her. I did, and she paced me to the finish. That got me to my first age-group ultramarathon win. On a birthday of her own, Catra ran for a mind-blowing forty-nine hours.

I went into the Wildwood challenge feeling confident. I had run thirty-one hours before on more challenging terrain, so I knew I had it in me. But my birthday, in late May, happened to fall on a rainy week in Portland, and it poured the entire time I was on the trail. The path became so muddy that my run turned into more of a controlled fall, testing my balance with every step. I couldn't get into my comfortable and familiar long-distance running groove.

After running forty miles in these conditions, it grew dark. My feet were waterlogged and sloshing in my shoes. I had developed all sorts of new blisters under these wet conditions. My muscles were shot from trying to stay upright. But ultimately, it wasn't the mud that got to me. It was nighttime. It was the darkness.

Running an organized race, you have aid stations. Every few miles you can see a light in the distance and know you can make it there. You have pacers. There is food and warmth and blankets along the way, places to dry off and people to hand you a hot chocolate. All I had now was a deep midnight before me, and I was horrified by how quickly it swallowed me up in a sense of despair.

What the hell am I doing out here all by myself? I wondered. The senselessness of my goal confronted me with every footfall. I was jumping at every noise and flinching at every corner, slowly allowing my fears to consume my thoughts and stir my imagination.

In my exhaustion, I bent over and laid a hand on the ground. The dark mud oozed through my fingers and under my nails. I saw that the mud had also covered the backs of my legs; streaks of dirty rain and grit dribbled down my calves. The wind whipped through the trees beside me, lashing them around like they were weightless and threatening to toss me farther down the trail. It poured and poured. I wanted to join the sky with my own tears, and at that moment I knew that night had won.

When I'm scared, I find myself turning to my past experiences of overcoming fear. The most scared I have ever been on a trail run was at the Grand Canyon's Rim to Rim to Rim challenge. In one day, a group of us ran from the South Rim to the North Rim, and back again, a distance just shy of fifty miles. At first, it was glorious. I saw the sunrise over the rocks, the patient mules trudging down the trail, and the orange sand dusting my shoes. I bounded along like a carefree deer, thrilled to my core and grateful beyond words. Then, on the final climb up Bright Angel Trail – with seven miles to go – darkness fell. The animals started to come out, and I spotted the glowing eyes and outline of a mountain lion for the first time in my life. Bugs buzzed around my headlamp, attracted to its bright beam, and this attracted the bats. For miles, hungry bats would swoop down inches from my face to catch their dinner.

When I sat down to take a break, I realized that the ground was swarming with dozens of tiny scorpions. Whenever I stopped, they rushed toward me. I crawled out of that canyon exhausted and grateful to be alive. My nerves were shot.

★ ★ ★ ★ ★

I did get a big dose of Alaska fear on our visit, not on the highway, but on the Mount Marathon Race course in Seward. The race itself is not a marathon distance. It's an infamous 5K from the edge of town to the top of 3,022-foot Mount Marathon and back that takes place every Fourth of July. To say this course is mountainous is an understatement. Essentially, it is a cliff.

Every year, four-hundred men, four-hundred women and two-hundred juniors line up for the grueling summit and descent. The average speed uphill is 2 mph. It's more like bouldering than running. Downhill, speeds average 12 mph. Paramedics wait below to receive the bloodied and banged up finishers. Emergency crews are also positioned mid-summit to pull off the runners in severe distress. In 2012, a Mount Marathon runner from Anchorage disappeared on the course. He just … disappeared.

As crazy as this race sounds, my genius mind came up with the idea of doing it alone since we had missed the race date. This is how I found myself clinging for dear life off the side of a cliff with nobody around to hear my screams. Flies swarmed my bare arms and legs, tearing off mouthfuls of my skin and feasting happily by the hundreds. With all my limbs clinging to the cliff, I had no way of swatting the flies and frankly they were the least of my worries. In my desperation, I started to pray, repeating just four simple words, "Don't let me die." When I finally got to the bottom, I didn't care that I hadn't finished the complete course. I ran back to the RV and sighed deeply. I knew I had been stupid and risked too much.

I read articles about night running safety, and realize I am doing everything wrong. For example, I don't always run with a buddy and I don't run under bright streetlights. I seek out the deepest, darkest corners where the monsters live, and that's where I go. Still, the risks are calculated and I'm usually willing to live with the worst that could happen. Even stronger than my fear of an attack is my fear of staying indoors. I don't want things to be easier.

This is the drive that helped me complete three one-hundred-mile races – a distance I strongly associate with night running – in one year. And make no mistake: Running through the night *is* the hundred-miler. It sets these races apart from any other. In a fifty-miler or a 100K, you can finish and sleep in your own bed that night. In the hundred, there is no rest. You are forced to face your monsters head on, and they come out in the dark.

Nighttime for me usually comes at mile sixtieish. I have already been on my feet since sunrise and I am looking at a long night of running ahead. If I am lucky, I will finish shortly after the sun rises the next day. If I struggle, I will swelter in the heat and hope to finish before the afternoon sun burns off the last of my will. It's an experience for which you can't completely train. It's also tough to mentally prepare for, because the iron-like mind you begin with turns to mush at mile fifty, sixty or seventy when the darkness hits and your nightmares come alive. It's hard to prepare for the mind games, the sleep deprivation, the hallucinations.

In Greek mythology, Nyx is the goddess of the night. She is said to possess exceptional power and beauty, yet she has only ever been seen in glimpses. Her daughters are known as the Maniae. They are a group of spirits that personify insanity, madness and crazed frenzy. For the ultrarunner, night running and madness do indeed go hand in hand, one giving birth to the other. The hallucinations are the worst. They hit you at the peak of exhaustion and sleep deprivation. Although afterward you can laugh about them, when they are happening they're a nightmare you can't wake up from. In my first hundred-mile race I saw terrifying scarecrows and at one point I nearly cried, convinced that an enormous rattlesnake was on the path. There was nothing there.

When finishers talk about completing a hundred-miler, sometimes they say that they finished strong. Many of them have a good first fifty miles. But I have never heard anyone say, "Man, I rocked that night section!" On the contrary, runners talk about getting a second wind when the sun comes up. They talk about hanging on through the night. They remember wishing hard for the sun to rise or telling themselves if they can only get through the night, they might pull off a finish.

But there are lessons to learn running at night, and I strive always to be a student of the darkness. This is where I learn what I am made of – what remains when nobody is around to see me or hear me or praise me. It is a true test of heart and mind. At every hundred-miler, there is a breaking point of exhaustion where my fears surrender and my mind transforms.

I once wrote that I run one hundred miles because it's the only thing I do that demands my all. I need some things in my life to be hard. I need some things to demand more of me, to insist on everything, until all that is left is a raw strength of will, the power in my legs to keep churning out the miles, and the focus of my mind to reach my goal.

That's the thing about night. Some days it can grace us with cool air and spectacular sunsets, with stars so numerous that we question our significance and a moon so brilliant we think we can reach out and touch the universe. Then other days it turns in rage and abandons us. We are left feeling cold and lonely, just a vast nothingness. It can turn our souls into shallow, empty shells. Once the sun goes down, anything can happen.

Yet no matter how treacherous the night is, there is always this glimmer of hope: that in only a matter of time, the sun will rise again. And that is what night running has taught me about life. Some nights will be blissful and cozy with comforting dreams. Others will be sleepless, seemingly endless and full of terrors. But the sun will rise on them all if I am only brave enough to confront my worst nightmares.

Before I started running at night and before I knew about ultramarathons, I had different fears. I was scared of instability, hunger, emotional and physical abuse. I dreaded not being able to have children. I was afraid of not being noticed or being noticed too much. Above all, I was worried I would never find my place in this world.

Today my place is on the trails. I can be myself without fearing abuse or reprimand. I still have fears, but they are different. My friend and fellow ultrarunner Mike Miller wrote, "Dying in the woods does not frighten us. What frightens us are cities and paperwork, car crashes and sitting on a sofa watching TV. We fear dying a long, slow death trapped in a bed, and becoming a financial and emotional burden to our loved ones." Like Mike, I am terrified by complacency, conformity and compromise.

★ ★ ★ ★ ★

At 11 p.m. it is bright as day in the Yukon. My boyfriend and I are parked alongside the Alaska Highway at a secluded pullout near an untouched lake. We are the only human intruders for miles. Mountains tower in the background while beavers leap off a nearby rock and glide carelessly by.

We hear the cracking of twigs and spin around just in time to see the distant outline of a massive moose drinking calmly at the water's edge. The water is so clear that I can see the bottom. I am filled with a wild impulse to strip naked and swim with the dog. While I normally feel a sense of belonging in nature, here I stumble along like a tourist in a euphoric stupor. Of all the living things that surround me, I am quite possibly the slowest runner.

It's midnight and the sun is finally starting to set. I smile into the sunset as I realize that I have traveled farther north than anyone I know. Although I am not the first to walk these lands, I am the first of my kind. I have broken new ground beyond what was expected of me. I have not conformed. I close my eyes and take a deep breath. I have everything I need right in front of me: a mountain, an ocean, fresh air and my dog. I pull on my running shoes and my heart draws me to the road ahead. In this moment, I am not afraid of anything.

STEVE KETTMANN, a former columnist
for the *Berliner Zeitung*, is the author most
recently of *Baseball Maverick: How Sandy
Alderson Revolutionized Baseball* and *Revived
the Mets*. He lives in Soquel, California.

ALONE WITH
THE DINOSAURS IN
EAST BERLIN

BY STEVE KETTMANN

The echoing concrete stairwell was pitch black and that was how I wanted it. I closed the door to Sarah's and my third-floor Berlin apartment behind me and started down the steps with no thought of hitting the light button. What would be the point? It was closing in on midnight and I was going for a long run. How would it help me to light up the steps? Better to adjust to the dark. I kept the fingers of my right hand fanned out against the rough-fabric wallpaper lining the stairwell and marked my steady progress. Back in the high-rise student dorms at Berkeley years earlier I'd made a habit of jumping eight steps at a time and flying down the stairwell on pace to beat the elevator. Now I was taking the steps one at a time. Finally I was through the swinging front doors of our apartment building and out into the East Berlin summer night.

Traveplatz across the street was exploding with foliage. The trees whose glazed, sad limbs I stared past all winter were pushing out their fresh unfurling greenery like flea-market vendors hawking their wares. Their presence was almost claustrophobic. It felt good to get under way, early steps slow and expectant, arms swinging easily. I ran southwest toward the Spree River that cuts through the middle of Berlin like a '70s-wide belt cinched up tight, and from the sidewalk marveled at how much my adopted city had changed.

When Sarah and I moved in two years earlier, back in Berlin after our years together in New York and Madrid, the space on the corner had contained some throwback-to-East Germany "co-op" kind of place. It was always gloomy dark inside and the shelves I glimpsed through opaque windows were always bare and dusty and decades past needing fresh paint. Now on this corner was a trendy café, Aunt Benny, smartly laid out by a former design student from Canada, where English and estrogen filled the packed, bustling interior at all hours.

I was in the realm of street lights, but not for long. Once I cleared a few blocks of apartment complexes, video-rental stores and Mexican and Vietnamese restaurants, I would reach the open fields near the river and then I would be running in the dark for the first time. I'd barrel down tree-shrouded trails where in daylight the uneven surface led me always to focus hard on every footfall lest I rip, twist or tweak something and that now at night would be ink black. It sounded great. The best part was I had no idea how I'd happened on the notion of going for a run despite it being the dead of night.

Sarah was down in the Balkans, soon after completing her master's dissertation at Berlin's Free University on Kosovo's VETËVENDOSJE! self-determination movement, which meant I was left to fend for myself with the awkward duties of hosting my sister and her husband on their first visit to Berlin. Jan and Don and I had shared an enjoyable day, taking advantage of the weather to walk for hours. I'd shown them the crazy hulking forms of the Soviet War Memorial tucked away in a corner of Treptower Park where few tourists ventured (unless they happened to be Russian). We'd had pizza by the square at my favorite little spot in the Bohemian, multicultural West Berlin neighborhood of Kreuzberg and ventured into the crazy free-for-all of *Görlitzer* Park, a Berlin version of People's Park in Berkeley, where music and pungent smells filled the air at all hours. By the time we got back to the apartment after dinner and had a last glass of wine, we were all relaxed and content. Conversation was rolling along nicely until my sister remembered something.

"Oh right," she said, smiling at Don. "It's our anniversary! That means we're going to have sex!"

Good for them, but one thing was clear: I had to get out of there. But what could I do with myself? I wasn't hungry, nor did I have the urge to hit any bars. A crazy impulse came over me: What about going for a run in the dark? I couldn't do *that*, could I? I posed the question to myself, half-aloud, as I leaned over the bathroom sink and popped in my contact lenses. I asked it again – *could I?* – as I yanked on my running gear. The question floated along with me as I veered into a small park along the Spree and in the dark gloom started to pick up more speed. *Could I?*

* * * * *

I was never a runner. It feels like someone else's memory, implanted in my head via a silicon chip, but I have a sense that sometime just after college my brother Dave and I *did* run a 10K along the fake shores of some landfill community on the San Francisco Bay. That would have been about 1985. Back then running for me was all about overestimating myself. Dull and boring things like regular training or an easy stride were for other people. I'd just push through the pain and charge up a steep incline in Berkeley along a fire trail. I'd go hard and hurl, then go hard again. It was an approach that was all about self-limitation and self-delusion. Doing that one and only 10K of my pre-forty-five running days, I went out hard and flamed out hard, ending up having to walk the last half-mile. I think I blamed my failure on someone or something. Sounds like my twenties in a nutshell.

My new approach to running started with a 2002 ferry ride across the Strait of Gibraltar. I developed a peculiar compulsion that day, staring down at the churning Mediterranean, to swim from Spain to Morocco. At that point maybe a hundred or so people had done it, at least officially. I started training and looked for a partner. My longtime friend Pete Danko, a roommate back at Berkeley, laughed off the idea. The next year I tried again: What if I, never a runner, somehow completed a marathon with him? Would he in turn agree to swim Gibraltar with me? Entertained by what he reasonably saw as the certainty of my spectacular failure, he told me we had a deal.

I had to laugh at the crazy unlikelihood of it all. And I kept smiling right through the entire transition from guy who found it a challenge to do five laps around the little square out front to guy who ran half-marathons. In no sense did I burn with desire to turn myself into a hardcore runner. In no sense was I intent on success. I was not about to turn the whole thing into some kind of stupid personal boot camp, or torment myself with schedules or instructions. I was not going to push myself to run faster or run harder. I would cajole myself into getting my ass out the door, yes, but that was as far as I'd take it: I wanted running to feel as much like work as taking a bath. I kept this comparison in mind when I followed up an hourlong run with half an hour in the bath.

I found that as I focused more and more on keeping it free and easy, something strange started happening during my runs. My body started to make choices on its own. I would slowly pick up speed without even noticing it. My stride would lengthen. The world would fade away. I'd be left with a feeling like being on one end of a rubber band tugging me forward. It felt good. I liked that sense of being pulled along. Oh, if I started thinking too much about what was happening, sometimes the mood vanished. I would suddenly become aware of the people around me and the tweaks and twangs in my legs that had been of zero interest to me just a moment earlier. But mostly once I got in a zone I stayed there. I started seeing one run as an extension of the next.

Sometimes I had the sense as I was running that the movement was really a disguised version of dancing. Other times I just let myself enjoy the feeling of being outside, far from any computer screens or deadlines, free to suck in fresh air blowing over the Spree. The night before I ran my first half-marathon in a scenic corner of Bavaria called Altötting I stayed up late reading Haruki Murakami's *What I Talk About When I Talk About Running*. The book inspired me as a runner and as a writer to spend less time wondering what I might be able to do if only, if only, and more time just doing it. Murakami believes that a writer can build stamina through running, stamina that serves us well during the inevitable times when fear and doubt nip at our heels or exhaustion brings us down. A sense of discovery beckons to both writer and runner, if you can only calm the fears and keep on going, and going, and going.

★ ★ ★ ★ ★

I kept glancing up at the tall Gothic lamps spaced out every so often on the trail gently curving through the gloom of the Plänterwald. Up to this point night running had been almost disappointing in its lack of drama. I was amazed at the feeling I had of my feet and legs knowing the way all on their own without much input from me. I'd come through the little park fronting the Spree and headed up over a railroad bridge toward Treptower Park with a postcard view of Berlin's comic TV Tower, the iconic Fernsehturm, looming a few miles downriver, its dimpled dome making me smile with *Jetsons* associations. As an American living in Berlin I never got tired of looking at the TV Tower and feeling pulled back into the past. It was as if it were October 1969 again and Communist Party leader Walter Ulbricht was celebrating the twentieth anniversary of the German Democratic Republic by all in one day marking the opening of the Fernsehturm and then throwing a switch to bring color television for the first time to GDR residents.

I had run about four miles, the last of it along a pebbly stretch of tree-bounded trail that was completely dark, when for the first time I had a sense of foreboding. I could hear snickering and something like caterwauling up ahead. I kept my eyes moving, not really scanning, since when you're looking around in the dark you really don't see much of anything, but keeping them moving anyway, just in case. As I kept running I caught glimpses of the glow of a fire, ten meters back from the trail, and of forms huddled around, clinking beer bottles and making the loud, growling sounds that for some reason young German men with beer in their bodies like to make. It was an unnerving sound, even if it was also embarrassing in its achingly transparent youthful attempt at appearing tough.

I laughed, but I'll admit my heart rate picked up. I had so loved the feeling of being alone in the quiet night, these revelers felt like a small violation. Then I was past them and it all seemed so stupid. They didn't care about me. I didn't care about them. Losing yourself in a run meant never having to care about any of that, since you could always throw it into a sprint and be gone. In night running what normally alarms you might soothe you instead and what would soothe you most of the time might seem suddenly alarming. In almost no time, as I ran deeper into the dark along that riverside trail, the fire and the rowdy little group flickered into a point of recollection and then vanished.

I had never felt my feet the way I did that night. A good golfer, like my brother Dave, will read a putt with the feet as much as with the eye: Standing there on an undulating slope, the feet feel nuances of contour the eyes would miss. I found myself thinking about Dave as I kept running. I realized that running at night felt easier than running during the day when my eyes were forever peering down at this divot in the path or that protruding brick face. At night I just let my feet tell me what to do. They somehow knew. They somehow felt with each footfall where the next foot should land.

I had only one more stretch of tree-canopied trail where I'd be running in total darkness before I reached the realm of electric light again. A sudden rustling sound to my right made me jump to my left. Whatever was moving was not small. This was not the tapping of small animal paws. But with a single rush whatever had been there was gone, retreating from me faster than I could retreat from it. Again I had to laugh at myself and the impulse toward fear. The scariest animals I was going to see on this night run were lifeless: Through the ivied-over wire-mesh fence dividing the riverside trail from the surrounding forest loomed giant forms from the Triassic period.

A strange little amusement park complex had been built here in the Plänterwald in 1969 during the heyday of the East German state. A few huge fiberglass dinosaurs remain to this day and on the dark run I could just make out the form of a drooping brontosaurus, its face daubed with white paint in some failed attempt at a witty post-graffiti commentary. The dinosaurs were my landmark, telling me I'd reached the point where I'd soon be through to the wide fields leading to a promenade along the Spree, where house boats floated next to little huts selling bratwurst with a bridge looming in the background that would carry me home. I was totally alone, just me and the dinosaurs, and it felt great.

The dark woods enveloped me, a gauzy protective layer keeping me remote from any concerns of what might be happening anywhere in the world other than right here. I'd reached a place in the dark where the rubber-band feeling I'd learned to love was not just strong, was not just present, it was all there was. I could feel it pulling me ahead. A run could become a trapdoor drop into a state of feeling both calm and powerful, a feeling that I could run all night long, until the first light of day seeped into the Berlin distance and broke the spell. It was a feeling I never wanted to end.

DAHLIA SCHEINDLIN, an international public
opinion researcher and political strategist,
has consulted on campaigns in more than a
dozen countries. She was raised in New York
City and currently resides in Israel.

RUNNING TO THE INTERIOR

BY DAHLIA SCHEINDLIN

S trangers are the meaning of my life. My job is to rush into other countries, or dive into my own, and delve inside the brains of total strangers. As a public opinion analyst sent to do fieldwork on multiple projects in various countries at a breakneck pace, the main challenge is how to do everything fast: For years I was rushing to catch planes, hurrying through hours and hours of people talking, watching streams of words rushing by me. My job then required me to jump into the stream and catch them, to stop everything in order to feel how these people feel in a suspended moment of familiarity – then extract the ideas, put them into new words, write them up and send them on. After that, I'd run on to the next project, often in a different country, city or village with only days or hours in between assignments.

It became clear, without my ever articulating it to myself or anyone else, that if I was going to be able to journey into the minds of others, I could not lose sight of myself. With the daily pressure and the profound responsibility, I nearly gave myself over completely – almost. Perhaps it was a survival instinct, but even when life was running past me so fast, I made a point of saving an hour for my own private running – not for some strangers whom I had to interview for my job, but for myself. Sometimes it meant I set my alarm for the middle of the night, even if I was in a place I had never been and did not know, like a remote corner of Bulgaria that was unfamiliar to me in every way. Those runs became a way of preserving my soul.

I hadn't counted on the darkness. Arriving in the town of Lovech the previous day, I'd learned that there was only partial electricity. The information registered as an abstraction, like a fact in an encyclopedia; now I was confronted with the reality. I stepped out into the murky chill of predawn rural Bulgaria and felt what it means to live without lamplight. Not just that: There were no signs, no markers, and for me, still the stranger, no landmarks. All I had were these forty-five minutes and a pair of running shoes to claim something – was it time, space, or some other unknown? – for myself. These were my only paths back to the person who was not a stranger, buried somewhere beneath all the layers of labor and exhaustion.

I stepped out. To my right was a covered bridge leading to the other side of town. To my left was a road, not sufficiently paved to be considered a street. The darkness was huge and silent but in the moment it took to survey the options, the outline of the road became clearer. Perhaps it was the only thing, for a moment, that could be seen. It seemed to lead upward, as if climbing into the mountain. I headed to the left, unsure of what it would mean to take this dark path, but somehow I felt I trusted this road. I believed the road welcomed me.

★ ★ ★ ★ ★

All activity, in a way, can be divided into two types: There is the kind that resides within the boundaries of a single human body or mind, reaching downwards and perhaps uplifting, but remaining inside. It's not exactly a monologue because there is a dialogue with that very self – not in a schizophrenic way, or not necessarily, but in the way that human beings have of asking themselves questions, Socratically, to play out the truths that we know are inside us the deeper we go. Then there are the activities that burst outward, that reach out and embrace someone else – a human being, a pet, a tree. These are the activities of communication, that great basis of life: talking, laughing, fighting, eating, singing, touching, screwing up or being ridiculous.

Human nature is biased toward the latter. We are built, according to all the psychological studies, to be social. Yet so much of modern life enables aloneness. We can be surrounded by bodies, busy at jobs that purport to need us desperately and command that the cellphones must always be on, the inboxes always open; we can live in the middle of a dense urban space, in an apartment surrounded by many others, on a planet bursting with people, within a family forever intruding, and still be very alone.

My job made me feel important: The machines were always looking for me. I flew business class and stayed in fancy hotels where everything was gleaming and the bellboys and maids and room service attended to me around the clock. But who was I? I moved from country to country at a dizzying pace and in each country I plunged anew into the culture and the very minds of the people. In a way it was work that suited me: I love thinking about people and wrestling with all the aspects of human nature I can find to consider. But I was a slow-burning soul in a fast-paced job; there was so much stimulus that I hardly had a chance to take it all in before rushing along to the next task, the next group of interviews, the next city, the next country.

Returning home, there was no way to explain everything, to communicate it all to any one person. It was just too much. And once I made it back, I was immediately busy with the next thing and the next after that. Days and documents rushed by; big stacks of material would flood the inbox for one project while I was working with my other hand on two reports that needed to be churned out by yesterday. Everything else in my life became a form of maintenance. I congregated with friends to catch a breath of my soul outside of work. I gathered enough food to keep healthy.

I ran because it was my anchor. I ran no matter how I was feeling or what time the running had to be done to fit into my day. It's strange to describe the particular inner world of running because it was the only part of my life that did not need to be articulated. Everything else was words – work and play – but running was silence. A metaphoric silence, deeper than the music that might or might not accompany me. It became the only moment when I was alone but not lonely; thinking without explaining; feeling without justifying the feelings, editing them, or making sense of them at all. It didn't matter how I looked or how other people saw me. Running was a bridge between the deepest, most real points of myself, a way of connecting them to the vast world beyond the borders of this body.

Then the day would start. I'd find myself on an airplane, in an airport, at a customs line, trying to cut through new-country bureaucracy, while remembering the long list of new facts, ideas and developments I had read on the way there, fighting sleep during those early morning flights that brutally severed my nights, all the while searching through the sleepy fog for a taxi that was not driven by a huckster. Sometimes I would gaze down at the ground from the flight and test myself to see if I remembered where I was going, or if I could figure it out from the ground below.

There was no way to figure out Bulgaria from the ground below. I had been to some remote places – an oil rig in the North Sea, rural villages in Zanzibar – and found points of entry, a way to relate to the country. But Bulgaria was yielding nothing. It was thirteen years after the fall of communism in 1989, but I found the people reticent, the rooms barren and cold, and nothing seemed to be working. Buildings literally crumbled as I walked by them on the street. There was something more than the language barrier. I felt that even when the people of this country talked to each other, there was something stilted and wooden about the conversation.

Touching down in the capital city of Sofia, I plowed through an exhausting work day. From there I was jettisoned to other parts of the country, working feverishly during the days to concentrate on political conversations for five hours at a time. At night I'd return to the hotel room for more work. Around midnight, I would drift off over the keyboard and curl up on a sofa, keeping a careful distance from the bed, in order to gather energy to keep writing in short spells, fighting off sleep. Then around 3 or 4, I'd crawl into bed with the lights on, so as not to really sleep, and wake up at 5:30, to take my body through forty-five minutes of activity in the brittle air.

For two nights, I had the strangest sensation during those two hours of near-sleep: In a tiny bed in a tiny room in a tiny hotel in the littlest towns in Bulgaria, I felt a sensation creeping over me like nothing I'd ever experienced; it was the first time I'd ever had to deal with genuine symptoms of protracted sleep deprivation. Waves of strangeness coursed from my toes to my stomach and washed through my head, rising and falling like a noise between my ears, through my half-sleep. My mind was distorted and my body was laughing and falling. In the confusion of near-sleep, I was sure there was a sort of madness taking hold, so strange that it could never be identified and maybe had no cure. Would I ever come out of it? I lay like this for two hours each night, in terror and awe of these unfamiliar sensations.

On the third or fourth night – they started to bleed together – we arrived in Lovech. Other places had been geographically distant, but Lovech, 150 kilometers north of

Sofia, felt farther away than I'd ever been, from anything I'd ever known. It had no Internet connection and parts of it didn't have electricity. And it was freezing. It did have a covered bridge, of which my Bulgarian colleagues were very proud, but this meant little to me amidst the hazy eyes of sleeplessness and overwork. I did what I had been doing – got through the tasks of the day, retired to my tiny hotel room, more like an inn, to write and avoid sleep. We had to move on early the next morning, and so again, my alarm was set for some early hour long before sunrise. This is how I came to be facing such a foreign scene, alone in the predawn quiet. But cutting through the fog of exhaustion, the chill of the mountains, the strangeness of the language and the stony mood of the people was a flicker of familiarity: I was ready to run.

I stepped out, gasping at the first breaths of air, shocking my lungs with the cold. There was nothing to guide me but the darkness. But the darkness, it seemed, drew a line for me, in dust or black, beneath my feet as they ran. It was the road, and I could always see the road. Then to my right, I could make out a stream. Was it a river or a creek? In my memory, it was a stream, running like me despite the frozen temperature, modest in width and not angry or overflowing. Like the darkness, it was there for me as I ran, providing a guide. With the stream, I knew that even if I lost the unpaved road, there would be a clear direction back. I felt safe against confusion and free of fear, free of everything – they can have my body and even my mind, but my freedom is here, on this black and shining road.

Sure enough, the road turned up. Not left or right, it

simply began climbing the mountain. And it was beautiful. My feet drifted along; the trees were my friends, the nighttime knew I was there and in a way, I felt it was pleased that someone was out there to notice this most forsaken of places. I ran blind, knowing nothing of the step ahead of me, and felt protected.

Of all I had been told the entire previous day about the village, only one point of pride stood out: the bridge connecting the two sides of the river. The eyes of the locals shone like early morning moonlight when they spoke of the bridge. They crossed the bridge to find entertainment at night, moving over from the medieval past to the part of town that was about thirty years behind the modernity I was used to. They were waiting for something better, but taking pride in the past. Ultimately the past did not keep them there and when better things could be had, they left. More than six thousand of those who were there then in 2002 are gone now, some died perhaps – others moved on.

Up there on the road, in the rush and beauty of the night, alone on a faraway hill, I felt something about the town – and maybe the country – that had eluded me. Running through the shadows of the virgin valley, I felt that I was part of its existence, and lived with its people, felt what they felt. For those silent moments, running was my bridge to them, as well as to myself.

★　★　★　★　★

The bout of breakneck work and exhaustion finally ended a day or two later, topped off by an enormous meal. Then began the trip back to "civilization." To Sofia. Here, too, the night was so cold that I fled to the cocoon of my hotel room, with blasting hot air and a television through which I saw bombs exploding back in Israel, a reminder of the Intifada, the world I'd left behind. In this cold, insecure city, where I had no connection to anyone or anything, not even a favorite restaurant, I flipped television channels and was astounded to find two stations from my home country. Suddenly, all seemed right with the world! I laughed and cried through the advertisements, I was glued to the news, despite its terrible nature.

Actually, at the time, the country of Bulgaria remained fairly inconceivable to me. At the time, I was searching for a point of contact and found almost none, except perhaps in that windswept valley, rushing down from the mountainside covered with snow so pristine it glowed; perhaps in that wide, shallow river, bubbling under the light of a very large moon over a dark road, darker than I'd ever seen. I never knew the dark at all, it seems, until I saw this road by the moonlight before morning with no lamps. But the moment of moonlight before the first eastern rays were good enough for my body, clenched with cold as it strode through the air, breaths filling the space with clouds. All these years later, so many trips to Bulgaria since then, this remains my first and truest memory of that country. My feet had brought me home, to a place where I could also be at home in a no longer foreign land.

HEATHER SEMB, a former resident intern
at the Wellstone Center in the Redwoods
writers' retreat center in Northern California,
is preparing to hike the Pacific Crest Trail.
This is her first published essay.

ESCAPING AN INTERVENTION

BY HEATHER SEMB

I let the front door pull itself closed behind me as I stumbled through the entry way, kicking off my flats in disarray, not knowing or caring where they'd land. I just wanted to get home. I just wanted to retreat into the comfort and finality of my bed, free from obligation and empty conversation. These were the thoughts that streamed through my brain during the last few agonizing minutes of work, and a half-hour after clocking out and speed-walking home with my head down, desperate for some sweet relief from my loathsome attitude toward the world around me, I was able to feel something like happiness at the sight of the front door of the place I called home.

I had convinced myself that I was trapped in not one but two worthless jobs paying not enough to sustain me through a meaningless existence. Everything seemed to cost a lot of money all at once; I was living that game. My life should be more than this! The thought nagged at me, mocked me. But there I was: Asking people the same repetitive questions eight hours a day, if they wanted paper or plastic or mashed potatoes or coleslaw. It was draining the life out of me, burying my creativity under a toxic mountain of tedium and corporate kowtowing.

I was mostly angry with myself for being there, letting life pass me by as I wandered through random customer service jobs, too exhausted to care. When I mustered an emotional response, I was deeply saddened by the human interactions that I witnessed every day. I couldn't help but pick up on the unquenchable greed and sickly manner that had become the norm for so many people. Perverted old men hit on me constantly, foisting an immensity of selfish unhappiness and discontent for their own lives on me, leaving me carrying the weight of many sad souls. This was my burden as a hardware store cashier and working the counter at KFC. People would unload their negative energy onto me and in return, I'd release forced smiles and "Have a nice day" through gritted teeth.

As I walked into the living room that night after work, I noticed that everyone was home and sitting calmly together. There was something planned that night that I hadn't known about. Sensing tension and potential confrontation, I made a beeline for my bedroom. Ryann's words caught me midstride. "Hey Heather, how was work?" That was it. The intonation in her voice gave it all away. The unusual high-pitched tone, trying to hide awkwardness, trying to break through to me.

What was coming? I didn't know, but could feel something alive in the room, dense with concern vibrating from each one of my roommates locked in place on the beat-out '70s sofa. I spun around slowly, trying to act super casual as the question directed toward me hung unanswered in the silence. "It was fine, shitty people, shitty job, ya know, the usual." I tacked an awkward soft chuckle onto my bland statement, an attempt to ease whatever situation I'd just walked into. A sigh. The shuffling of feet.

I studied them. All of them. Grace was looking away, an uncomfortable expression smudged across her face. Cody was peering down, very fascinated with the folding of his hands, it appeared. And Ryann was looking directly at me, her head inched diagonally as she slowly nodded and gave me a small smile. But her dark eyes betrayed her: I saw a sadness in them as she glanced from me to Cody and Grace next to her, clearly trying to assemble the right words.

"We've been meaning to talk to you for a while about something," she said. "You haven't been acting like yourself. I've noticed that you spend a lot of time in your room. You hardly ever leave the house unless it's for work. I know that you're busy with everything in your life but you seem different. You and I have been friends for years and I've seen you happy and I've seen you sad, but I've never seen you this … depressed."

There was a pause before she said that last word, a pause weighted with fear. I stood there and couldn't feel my face or anything else for that matter. I couldn't believe that this was happening.

"Is this a fucking intervention?" I demanded, my voice holding more venom and despair than the humor that I had intended to convey.

"Not in the official way but, yes, sort of. We're just worried about you. Please don't shut us out."

Ryann beckoned for me to join them on the couch, but I wandered halfway there and made a place on the floor. For the next hour I listened to what all three of them had to say and answered their questions. I explained as well as I could the feeling that there was something major missing from my life.

"It's not that work is so bad all the time," I confessed on the verge of sounding melodramatic. "It's the amount of time I have to spend there, that's the issue."

I let the words flow out of me, uncensored and full of truth. Ryann made a point to turn the conversation in a lighter direction, toward hope.

"In high school, you played soccer, you were always running around, going to practice, trying to improve your game. I remember you were happy then. When's the last time you did something that physically challenged you?"

I scoffed.

"High school. Two years ago. And I sucked at soccer. Second string. Benched almost every game."

She saw the non sequitur in my self-pitying protest.

"My point is, you were moving," she said. "You got your heart racing. Maybe you need something like that in your life again."

I knew she was right. During my years as a somewhat physically active kid, I'd learned to love the feeling of exhausting my body, the pull to expose myself willingly to the uncomfortable and unknown, to satisfy true hunger by eating a well-deserved meal after many calories burnt. I also knew that I had a different desire than most, something uncertain driving me in my state of existence. So I told myself, then and there, that I had just enough character and the requisite hint of madness to become a runner.

Raw to the world and reckoning for change, I vowed I would begin to make it happen the next day. There was little in the way of plan or structure. Just a determination to find a greater meaning. Maybe it was in my head all along and my friends had chosen – miraculously or brilliantly – the right moment to pull it out of me, but I decided to feed my instincts and dive into an activity as primal and ancient as the shape of our hands. I would run for my life, for the life I knew I could obtain.

★ ★ ★ ★ ★

As a newbie cashier with no seniority, I was constantly working the late shift. My car had broken down a few weeks before, damaged beyond repair. A window was smashed in on the passenger side and I'd neglected to have it fixed through the worst of November weather, making for some stormy times inside my vehicle. Mushrooms were growing under the seat, and not the psychedelic kind. So I had sold my well-loved car and become accustomed to walking to and from work, which I didn't really mind. Outside the work-car-home bubble, I noticed more of my surroundings and got a little closer to nature. I needed more of this.

When I got off of work the night after I had the talk with my roommates, I stood in the parking lot of Ace Hardware. The sky was getting dark. The street lights were beginning to turn on. I was hungry and cold and despite my vow to change, for a flicker of a moment nothing sounded better to me than Netflix and Chinese takeout in the warm confines of my bedroom. But I had made a promise to myself to instill change in my life. If I went back on my word now and returned to the warm embrace of all that was safe but unsatisfying, I knew my chances of ever making a lasting impact on my life journey would drift further out of reach.

I made it to the high school track and changed into the workout getup I'd brought with me in my backpack. The sky was a deep blackish-blue now, just a sprinkle of stars and a slivery moon visible up above woodsy Paradise, California, in the Sierra Nevada foothills. Nobody was out there. Of course nobody was out there. Who else in this small town had thoughts like these that would compel them into the night? In the emptiness I thought about everyone in their houses bundled up with blankets, family and friends. But I wasn't envious. Now that I was out there my quest had become very official. I allowed myself the self-congratulatory pleasure of feeling bad for those who dared not take risks in any way and were stuck without change or resolution. Comfort can place one in a false state of delusion, hesitant to instill change. I was out there in my own nexus of space and time, removed from the world yet connected to myself and everything around me.

I started at a slow jog, "White Wedding" by Billy Idol blasting in my headphones. I was feeling pretty excited because this was so new. Everything in my brain seemed to speed up and slow down all at once. It was as though years of adrenaline that had been building up inside me had been released. It turned out I wasn't too far removed from my memories of movement. Maybe we never really are, maybe they reside in our DNA, or in some corner of our brains or muscles, no matter our sloth. I recognized the mind-altering feelings and thoughts that physical exertion could bring. The fact that the sun wasn't up heightened the atmosphere. I'd been hibernating a long time and it was now my turn to run free into the wild, reveling in the intensity.

As my legs adjusted to the cold, I really started to move and I glided down the lanes on the track. Everything passing by was a vision to behold. Every color was vivid in the dark hues of the silent silhouettes engulfing every figure. First lap completed. I was there because I wanted to be there. Work was mandatory to make a living but running was an option I had chosen. I ran past my obstacles of the day. There weren't any ignorant teenagers that I had to point in the direction of the spray paint on aisle seven. Nowhere in sight were angry old women, thrusting expired coupons in my face, demanding to speak to a manager because dammit they earned their half-off potting soil. There was no one out there on the field who I needed to please. Am I free? I asked myself. This unfolding event felt like a discovery of something familiar and good about myself. I decided that I was free.

After two laps, I began to notice that actually a couple was out there with me, sitting in the bleachers on the opposite side of the main grandstand. That realization got me thinking about a few years earlier, when I'd meet up with a boyfriend, stolen nights from our past lives. There I was, running in the nighttime, listening to music and feeling nostalgic. The couple would be cheering for the visiting team, if there was a sport in play. Hooray for the underdogs. I felt that way. Running there at night. Trying to regain my integrity, to rediscover the satisfaction of knocking out a dominant opponent, my opponent, the powerful humdrum of a perfectly repetitive and drearily boring workaday life. My running that night was defiant. Somehow, I was rebelling against the jobs that held me captive.

Yeah, my thoughts were pretty out-there that first night that I ran. They bounced and raced and flew around. I wasn't yet able to collect them and turn my mind toward a meditative state; that was something I would have to practice. Images of scary things hiding in the dark came to me, causing me to stop, listen and collect my bearings. It wasn't that crazy a notion. Cougars and bears were common sightings there on the fringe of the feral Sierra. But I was mostly afraid of bad people. Bad people that could've followed me from work or bad people that were already out there doing whatever it is they were doing. I tried to show the world that I was brave but inside, I was afraid of a lot of things.

Soon, the couple's presence blended into the night. I noticed there were one or two other people scattered around the track, and found comfort in the numbers. There wasn't going to be some kind of attack. As I calmed down, I noticed that I could breathe for the first time in what felt like a long, long while. I started to sprint, outstretched limbs doing what they desired, and I could feel a wild smile forming on my face, like a golden retriever poking out an open car window happily gulping in the rush of air.

Very soon after, due to my being unaccustomed of late to strenuous activities and utterly out of shape, I slowed down to a jog. Then I stopped. I yanked out my earbuds in a careless way that I had been warned against. I closed my eyes and heard my heart beating in the core of my body. Picked it up with my ears listening, as they always do, but this time with a more conscious awareness. I noticed the coppery taste of blood in the back of my throat. My lungs weren't used to inhaling so much air all at once, over and over. I put my hands on my knees and looked down through my legs. Ah, the feeling of a good stretch. Like my calves, my comfort zone just needed that extra little stretch. That "extra," that push beyond the norm – I knew that if I incorporated it into my life regularly enough, it could make me more flexible and help me live a life bursting with purpose and energy.

Say what you will about "Hotel California" and the billion times it has been played on classic rock radio, beaten to clichéd pulp, but if you listen closely you'll understand the Eagles knew some things. I thought about that great line, "We are all just prisoners here, of our own device," and about the power we have to shape our own reality, demonstrated in full force by this simple run that had turned around my thinking. Through the pain and discomfort I had come to realize that I needed natural highs in my life, highs that could make me the hero of my own story, send me soaring. I couldn't remember the last time that I felt so alive.

It was time to go home. If I had a car, this would be where my physical adventure would've ended, with a prosaic denouement, a five-minute drive of a few miles. But the mushroom-growing car with the window was gone. I felt fine about that, even lucky. I began the journey home by jogging steadily away from the school and out onto the streets. With a light-loaded backpack resting on my shoulders, I was an urban traveler of some sort, darting onto sidewalks and leaping across random holes in the ground. I felt triumph as car headlights momentarily blinded me and sped past me in the nighttime scene. I was a victor, surviving the game of life, defeating the sadness that threatened to encompass my soul. Even in awkward and clunky '90s tennis shoes, I could pretend I was a female warrior running into battle against the evils of modern society that pursued me.

Yes, I still had to go to work in the morning. Yes, once there I would be just another peon in the vast multitudes. But I knew that afterwards I could always run, through the starry night, and gain strength and mental clarity. When I got home and into bed later that night, I was ready for sleep. I was deliciously tired and I had running to look forward to the next day. I could get off of work, let loose, and be free. Everything would be all right.

T.J. QUINN, a former Chicago White Sox and New York Mets beat writer, is an investigative reporter for ESPN. He lives in New Jersey.

ONE HEADLIGHT: FINDING MY STRIDE ALONG THE PALISADES

BY T.J. QUINN

By midafternoon in January, Manhattan buildings glimmer in the sun but the New Jersey edge of the Hudson River has fallen into shadow. New Jersey itself still feels daylight, but the towering stone Palisades that run north from the George Washington Bridge block the sun near the water, and reinforce the idea that New Jersey is always a little darker than other places. A paved road rises and falls in swells along a slim stretch of wooded land between the cliffs and the river, and I love to run there because of the anonymity and the isolation.

The longest run of my life, sixteen miles, came on that road in the premature Jersey dusk of late January. I ran with the thought that I was training for a marathon, a distance I was coming to believe I just might conquer despite everything. My doubt wasn't based on a lack of athleticism or mental strength. It was really a matter of my knees, and sure enough, that marathon was not to be.

My left knee is a tattered trophy that hobbles me but gives meaning to every step. It was reasonably healthy until February 6, 1996, when I crossed Harlem Avenue in Chicago to get my car, heading to pick up Chinese food, and a woman turned into the intersection and hit me with her 1988 Oldsmobile. The impact tore my left MCL, ACL and meniscus, and left an impact fracture on the lateral tibial plateau. I was a week away from beginning my assignment of covering the Chicago White Sox for the *Daily Southtown* and had to delay my trip to spring training in Florida ten days while the swelling subsided. I didn't have surgery to repair the knee until months later, and when I walked into the Sox clubhouse with a massive brace on my leg, most players had no reaction. But aging, silent designated hitter Harold Baines, whom I had never seen initiate a conversation with a reporter, sat on a stool at his locker and gave me a knowing glance.

"Cartilage?" he asked.

I nodded.

"It'll never be the same," he said, shaking his head.

I have torn the meniscus in my left knee several times and have had four surgeries to repair or remove it. I'm told that I'm down to about 10 percent of what I started with. I didn't actually become a runner until after three of those surgeries. In high school I played football, soccer and ran track as a sprinter. In college, I was an amateur boxer, fighting as a light middleweight at 156 pounds. I hated running anything more than a quarter of a mile. Mostly, I couldn't stand that much time alone with my brain. In my post-collegiate world, I was a smoker and an eater and swelled to 220 pounds, although I thought I carried it relatively well. Seven years on a baseball beat, eating In-N-Out Burger at 1 a.m., did me no favors. But a combination of factors broke me out of the sportswriter's inertia and got me moving. I had a cousin who lived with stage four rectal cancer for years until he died at the age of forty-four. Danny convinced me that the smoking had to stop, that I had to do anything I could to prolong my life. I also had a spectacular accident on the New Jersey Turnpike when I was thirty-seven, sideswiped by an eighteen-wheeler while we were going seventy miles an hour. My little Honda was destroyed. The truck's gas tank ignited and kept the Turnpike shut down for eight hours as a tractor trailer full of bread became a pyre of toast. I was uninjured, but lost any spirituality I had and entered an existential crisis that left me, for the first time, with a crystalline understanding that I was mortal and vulnerable and running out of time. Then I turned forty.

"Happy birthday," a close college friend texted me on the morning of my fortieth birthday. "Welcome to the other side. There's nothing to fear over here."

"Yes, but there's no way back, either," I texted back.

So I began to run. I had a number of friends who also started running when they turned forty, and we all felt, to some degree, a combination of haste and vanity. For me, though, part of running's allure was the pain. It would start from the first step with microscopic explosions of tearing tissue, but I learned that after a mile or two I could run through it. Every run was a victory. The weight came off rapidly and people noticed. I ran four miles for the first time. I ran five (and the next day was diagnosed with swine flu). I ran six. I began to enter races and found that my knee and I finished regularly in the top 10 percent.

Training in Central Park for a 2010 half-marathon, I knew I had torn something again in my left knee, and I finally did something to the right one. My orthopedic surgeon, Joseph Bosco, opted not to operate on the right knee because the tear was in "a good place," just under the kneecap. It may hurt, he said, but you will not injure yourself. He had given me the language I needed: If what I felt was merely pain, I could manage it. But the torn meniscus in the left knee had to come out. I had surgery No. 4 a week after the race.

In my view of the world as a place where something has to hurt for it to be meaningful, I took great pride as he gave me an arthroscopic tour of the joint.

"See this? All that crab meat?" he said. "That's what we call 'TBS.'"

Even his surgical staff seemed confused by the term.

"It means 'totally beat to shit.'"

After grinding away at the frayed tissue and showing me the large patches of bare, damaged bone, Bosco announced to his team, "Ladies and gentleman, Mr. Quinn just ran thirteen miles on this knee."

There were nods and hums of approval. He gave me a sheet with several photos from the surgery. I have shown it to unsuspecting house guests as though I was showing slides of the Great Pyramids. And then I repeat what Dr. Bosco said about me and I wait for the admiring looks. They always give me a look, all right, but the look doesn't say, "What manly fortitude you must have!" It says, "What is the *matter* with you?"

The result of it all is that when I do run, that nobly battered left knee hurts and swells, and the more I run, the more it hurts and swells. The right knee simply hurts. At greater distances, the pain can become a problem, throwing my body out of whack as I compensate for both it and the fact that my left leg, lacking most of the meniscus I was intended to have, is now slightly shorter than the other. I get a cortisone shot in my left knee maybe twice a year, but Dr. Bosco was clear: "Your running days are numbered," he said. Eventually the bone-on-bone pounding will take a toll and that knee will be replaced. In the meantime, as long as I can handle the pain, I can, and do, run.

* * * * *

I found the road accidentally. I sought new trees to leap and rocks to navigate along the Hudson and went searching for them from the Englewood boat basin, which is cut from the shore just a mile north of the GW Bridge. My first attempt at a trail run there led me into nearly impassable rocks, so I followed a stone staircase to a road that cut north from the boat basin, and continued on the pavement. My road. It was a discovery only in a personal sense; any semi-serious cyclist knows the road, as do a handful of other runners. But it became mine.

I learned my road in increments. The first fourth-tenths of a mile are a hill of run-on-your-toes steepness, where you forget about pace and mindlessly climb. At the top, the road mercifully drops and then winds and rises and falls gently, the Hudson on the right, a steep patch of brush to the left until it hits the rising stone. Cyclists whiz by like wasps, and when the occasional car crawls by, it feels like a bear lumbering through a picnic. My time is early on a Sunday morning, preferably in the rain. When it rains there are no bicycles, there is no sun, there are only occasional runners, who are often older and always serious.

I figured out that a stone bridge marked three miles. So another half-mile, just over another hill, was the turning point for a seven-mile run. A longer hill would bring me to eight. Beyond eight, everything was a personal record. The day I set out to do twelve, I had run about five miles when I came to a fork. To the left, I could see there was a steep hill that disappeared to the left. To the right, the road ran down toward the Hudson. I decided I'd rather save the downhill for later, so I took off to my left and climbed.

What I found around a bend after a hundred gentle yards was a sharper incline that went farther than I expected. With every turn it became steeper and I began to wonder if I could finish it. There was no healthy slap to my steps, just a shuffling scratch. I conjured scenarios to push myself forward. *What if this was the last mile of the Olympic marathon?*

What if I had to save one of my kids from a snake bite? What if my father was watching? What if there were Nazis?

I thought of the hill the future paratroopers of Easy Company had to run in *Band of Brothers*. If they can do it, I thought.... Then, after another hundred yards, with no end to the hill in sight, I revised that thought. Those guys were eighteen years old and they were training for war. I'm forty-three and I'm training for a 10K. But after a mile of what I later determined was a 10-to-15-degree pitch, it opened to the New Jersey State Police station in Alpine, an area that I knew having come from the other side. Something familiar. I reached six miles, punched a lap marker on my watch, and turned to run back, confident I could have led men on D-Day, snakes and Nazis be damned.

As my runs became longer, they became a greater imposition at home. My wife asked me if there was any reason I couldn't do my long runs on Mondays, instead of Sundays. My brain reacted the way almost any long-distance runner's would: Impossible. You do long runs on Sundays. But after thinking for a few seconds, I gave the only honest answer: No, there was no reason. There might even be a benefit: It would be the same road I had come to know by heart, but even more solitary.

On the Monday of my sixteen-miler, I got my kids out the door and headed to Englewood, but I was behind schedule. I was out of the car ready to go before I got around to doing the math: I didn't have time for more than twelve before I had to get to an appointment. I would feel rushed and pissed off and I wouldn't get the mileage I needed. So I got back in the car and decided I would do what seemed patently unappealing: I'd come back in the afternoon.

No area of my life involves as much planning as running does. I returned to Englewood at about 3:30. I had timed my meals as best I could during the day to make sure I had sufficient energy, but no stomach or bowel issues, eating a bowl of oatmeal about an hour before the run. I had a few packets of Gu, a hand-held bottle filled with Gatorade, nip-guards, my iPod shuffle (mostly my musical comfort food: Sam Cooke, Bruce Springsteen, Johnny Cash, the Beatles), gloves, a knit cap, my GPS watch. I put Vaseline on my face to protect against the cold.

It was about 38 degrees when I started, but the temperature would quickly drop. Sixteen miles should take me a little less than two and a half hours, I figured, which meant I would be returning to the boat basin around six. The sun would set just after five. I started running at 3:37.

At the start of my run I realized I had never been here this late in the day. Usually, especially during the summer months, I would begin my Sunday runs around 8 a.m. when the parking lot was empty, and return around 9:30 or 10 when it had filled and there were people sitting at the snack bar near the water. On a Monday afternoon in January the snack bar was closed for the winter, and I saw only a few cyclists bundled in bright, expensive togs. The road I had run on dozens of times was now slightly unfamiliar because of the fading light. I went over the first hill, into the gentle downhill that let my heart and legs recover.

For the first half of my run, it was about process. Gentle pace, good steady stride, only sips of the Gatorade, and not until I had been running for at least an hour. A packet of

Gu every forty-five minutes, don't litter, store the empty packet. For the first few miles, there were a few runners heading back to the boat basin. Nods or small waves to each other. There were a couple of cyclists heading out, but they soon passed me again heading back. About four miles down my road, eight since I started running, there was no one left. After another mile, I came to my *Band of Brothers* hill and could see the New York shore was now in shadow. My legs were heavy and I knew this run would be slower than my fifteen-miler two weeks earlier, but I went up with relative ease. At the top, all I could think about was getting my breath, about how close I was to finishing the hardest thing I would do the entire week. I reached the top, passed the police station – my breathing heavy, but in control – and ran to where the road met highway 9W. That point marked ten miles for me, with six to go to get back to my car. It struck me that six miles was still a fair ways to go. The aches that started in my left knee, my hip and my back would all increase. So be it. I reached the traffic light and turned around, getting a smile from woman in an SUV who must have known I had just come up the hill. It was a smile of sympathy and admiration and I absorbed it.

As any runner knows, going uphill is tough on the muscles, downhill is tough on the joints. Now I was headed downhill, ten miles behind me (and 10,000 more to go), aware of a throb in my knee, like a scream muffled by a pillow. I was far more aware of the growing dark. The road, the river and the sky were melting into the same granite gray, and I could see lights across the river from the top of Manhattan.

At the bottom of the hill, I saw that the gate to the road was now closed. Not a problem, as I could just run around it, and it meant I would see no cars on this dark stretch, which was good. But it also meant that the gate on the other end was probably closed. There was a chance my car would be locked in. A surge of urgency went through me. I wasn't worried at any point about not being able to finish my run, but I was worried that somehow I would be stuck. Suddenly I very much wanted the run to be over, but I fought the primary instinct I had, which was to run faster. That would only mean exhaustion and a heightened risk of injury. Besides, I tried to reassure myself, there's always a way out. Even if I had to wait for some cop to lecture and release me, I'd get home that night. Probably. I had food and drink in the car. I'd be just fine. Probably. But just the thought of being trapped was enough to take me out of the inner sanctuary of the run and stoke a primal sense of awareness. We're built to feel this way. The music in my headphones became distracting noise and I turned it down.

Twelve miles in, the experience had become completely alien. There was no light left from the sky. Everything to my right, where the Palisades rose, was black. A half-moon provided minimal light through the trees above me, but it wasn't enough to see more than a few feet ahead. To the left, tiny New York lights appeared and disappeared behind the dark of the trees. They were as inspiring and as irrelevant as stars; heat and light for someone else.

I had run this road dozens of times. I knew how far I had gone and how far I had to go from landmarks along the road. But I couldn't see them now. Every once in a while I pressed the light on my watch to see how far I had gone, but I was a pilot relying on instruments. I started to climb hills I had climbed over and over, but now could not see more than a few feet before the rising pavement disappeared into space. I couldn't set little goals along the way – *just get to that rock* – to get myself home. Each step was a prayer that I wouldn't hit a crack or a pothole or a rock that tumbled from the cliffs and a plea that at some point each of these hills had to end.

I was thrilled. I was sharpened by the pain in my knee, the stiffness I was starting to feel in my back, the mild danger of a dark road. I could hear my breathing and my feet on the pavement. At some point I could hear a rustling ahead on my right, and a bolt of adrenaline went through me. The sound grew louder, and it wasn't until I was next to it that I realized the sound was a waterfall I normally passed without paying much attention. There were maybe three miles left.

Two hills marked the end of my Sunday runs. One was manageable, but it plateaued only briefly before the last hill, the one that took me back to the first peak. With one tower of the GW Bridge visible to the left, I began climbing what I knew was the first hill. My legs were heavy, and the pain of my knee passed into numbness. The road flattened. Now the last hill, with relief only a few minutes away. I was on my toes again, unable to see anything but lights across the river. No end to the hill. The road was turning slightly to the left – I still couldn't see but I knew there were only a hundred yards or so to go. Then a glowing line ahead, the lights from Manhattan coming behind the hill, mindless movement of my arms and legs, my mouth wide open, and then the ground was flat again. There were four-tenths of a mile left, but the run was essentially finished. I wanted to sprint but could not, so I rumbled down the hill to the parking lot. There was another car, but I could see no one. I came to my dirty gray Prius, and stopped.

The Vaseline was gone from my face, replaced with a thin crust of salt. The film of fear was gone, too. As the primal brain went back into slumber mode, my modern brain came back to life in glorious self-awareness. For some reason, standing alone in a dark lot, I caught myself trying to look cool.

I stretched half-heartedly, drank with gusto, all part of a performance for no one. I checked my watch – much slower than my last run. I checked my phone, ate a banana, paced in the parking lot. My left leg was stiff and would barely bend, but I pictured the Aleve and the ice bath that awaited me at home. I started thinking about how I would plot out an eighteen-mile course in a week (a run that wasn't to be).

I also allowed myself a moment to note that in just a few years I had gone from struggling for three miles to cruising for sixteen. I had run the Palisades at night. I was more than my knee, more than the dark, more than anything that rustled in the woods. I was a conqueror. I slid into the car, turned on the radio, and slowly drove up the switchback. At the top there was no gate, nothing to stop me, and I merged into traffic to make the short drive home in the dark, one set of headlights among many.

★ ★ ★ ★ ★

Epilogue:

A couple of months after my father's death I was in London for work, and found that after a year (yes, a year) of plodding through a few pages at a time I had come to the end of James Joyce's *Ulysses*. Having no way to tell my father, I walked, and I found myself retracing a path he and I had followed twenty-eight years earlier. As night fell and a gentle late-March rain began, I kept walking, another wandering Irish Jew, until I finished a loop that I measured at thirteen miles, soaked, bone weary, sore in feet and knees, my head still churning. Back in my room there was an email reminding me it was the last day to register for the New York City Marathon. So I typed in my information and signed up – "yes I said yes I will Yes" – and then I slept for ten hours.

From the time I had given up my last marathon attempt, I had undergone a fifth knee surgery (wherein Bosco removed a bone chip that looked strikingly like a human skull). A running friend gave me a marathon training book that preached fewer miles on the road and more on the bike. The training went well. When it came time for anything more than sixteen miles, my previous limit, I went to the west side of Manhattan and ran along the Hudson. I gave up the hills and solitude of the Palisades for the flat, populated wonders across the river.

Two weeks before the race, I did my last "speed" workout: four 1,600-meter repeats around the Central Park reservoir for the sheer romance of it. In the middle of my last repeat, there was suddenly a tingling spot on the outside of my right Achilles tendon, as if someone had placed a warm stone there. A couple of days later, while running a triumphant eight miles on a treadmill, my last real run before tapering, a worrying tightness came and went. The next morning, I could barely walk. I sought Bosco's help, and began taking corticosteroids and wearing nitroglycerine patches on my heel to stimulate blood flow. It was tendinitis, he said. It was severe, but the tendon was not at risk of rupturing. "You'll be OK," he said. "You've done the work."

So for two weeks I stretched, took my medicine, limped slightly as I took my son on a college visit to my alma mater, and did not run. On marathon day, my daughter, fourteen at the time, set her alarm for 3:30 a.m. so she could send me a text before I left. This is what I awakened to:

> Heyyyyyy teej! You should probably be up by the time I send this..... And hopefully soon on your way to ny. I hope you got some sleep last night! I know you are feeling really anxious and a bit nervous..... But try to think about this.....

1. A few years ago you started running, and 2 miles was a struggle. But you worked your butt off, and increased your distance by A LOT.

2. You got up at times that aren't very pleasant to get up at... So you were ready to wake up your kids for school.

3. You work and work and coach and have pretty crazy busy kids and lots of responsibilities, but you always managed to work in time to run

4. You managed to try something you always saw as an unpleasant, and turned it in to something you love

5. You have had 5 knee surgeries, and you still manage to run!!

6. You decided you wanted to live a healthy life style and change your life for the better, so you did.

7. You worked hard.. And as corny as it may sound... You never gave up!!

The marathon is about to happen... And I am very very proud of you. Not because it sounds cool to say "my dad is a marathon runner" but because I know you worked so hard.

Hopefully your ankle will be able to bear it, but it's ok if it doesn't. It's kinda like how you tell me that what makes you proud aren't the grades I get, but all the hard work I put into it. No matter what happens, be proud of the work that you put in. You ran 20 miles already! Remember how in your essay you said 16 miles would be your longest run.... You already proved that wrong!

So when you are running try to remember that it is something you love... And something you taught me to love. Think of it as sticking up your middle finger to that dumb lady who hit you with the car

It's so cool that you are doing this and I am so lucky that I have you to look up to!

So best of luck teej!!! I love you soooo much !!!!

I ran to her room in tears, hugged her, and left. The rest of the day comes through only in patches when I look back: huddling with several French runners before the start, joking bilingually that we were like penguins, flapping our elbows by way of translation; the stiff northern wind on the Verrazano Bridge at the start; the noise of drums coming off the bridge into Brooklyn; running into my friend Tom Hill at mile 3. I felt a pinch in my left knee at mile 5 and smiled wanly, knowing that surgery No. 6 was now somewhere in my future.

As I took on the long, gentle slope leading up to the Queensboro Bridge, my balky right Achilles began to spark and soon I felt a raging fire spreading to the entire tendon. My mile splits slowed, from just over eight minutes to just over nine to ten and eleven and twelve and … fourteen. At Mile 17 my right knee had begun to swell, but my cousin Molly was waiting with a sign and a hug. At Mile 19 my left knee began to go. I could have used another hug. I felt the awful loneliness that I had felt only in dreams, wondering how I could ever cover so much ground ahead of me. I walked here and there, feeling a sense of failure, imagining I could no longer say I "ran" a marathon. My god, how long would it take to finish?

Finally I came to the park, passed Mt. Sinai, the hospital where I was born, and trudged down Fifth Avenue. By then my Achilles had gone numb, but the pain in both knees made it almost impossible to lift my legs. My shoes scraped the pavement. The young men who had accompanied me in the first miles had been replaced by old women with headphones. My goals had been reduced and tossed aside one by one like paper cups. I came up with one last one: I would not allow myself to walk during the last two miles.

I did keep running, and heard myself exhaling small grunts. My thoughts were frantic and desperate – *Where is the end? It has to end. There's always an end.*

25 miles.

26 miles.

26.2.

I stopped. I walked. I kept walking. I had no emotions. No pride. No fear. Certainly no joy. I could not feel my legs, other than a shapeless electric pain everywhere below my waist. I felt a hand on my shoulder. I turned. A woman I had not seen during the race said, "Great job." I looked at her and a sob escaped my mouth as I said, "My Achilles went at mile 15."

"Jesus Christ," she said.

I took my silver refugee blanket and my medal and my bag of free food and limped out of the park.

That, I expect, was the last race I'll ever run. My Achilles never fully healed. In June 2015 I developed a sharp pain in my back that turned out to be three discs bulging against my spinal cord. A neurologist looked at my MRI and told me I had "the neck of a runner." This was not a compliment, but a warning. In March 2016 I had that sixth knee surgery to remove a bone chip that had embedded itself under my medial meniscus. During the surgery, as Bosco showed me the barren landscape where there was no more lateral meniscus, he told me there was little more he could do for me. The battles I have waged against my body, the jousts with age and the standoffs with pain, will now be fought somewhere else. I have wrung out nearly every mile my body can provide.

Former Wellstone Books intern **KELSEY EILAND**,
a recent graduate of the University of California
at Santa Cruz, works at the UCSC Arboretum
and hopes to pursue a career in teaching.

10

LOST IN THE THAI COUNTRYSIDE

BY KELSEY EILAND

I just wanted to get home. Each unpaved, dimly lit back road began to look like the last. I could no longer see the neon sprawl of downtown Pattaya nor hear the whir of zooming motorbikes, the drivers yelling, "Taxi! Taxi!" The outskirts of town reminded me of a Thailand from decades past: stray dogs barking at passersby, exotic music streaming from late-night food carts, British expats murmuring broken Thai to their child brides. The stench of raw sewage began to permeate my sinuses, even as I was still catching wafts of fried fish and other street food. My lungs burned from a cigarette I had shared earlier in the night. With each step the thick, salty air felt heavier in my chest. My face grew more flushed as the pace of my breathing – *in, out, in, out* – accelerated.

How did I end up alone? I had been out with friends of friends whom I was staying with on the Gulf of Thailand. We all went out for drinks downtown in Dolphin Circle. Young Thai women, many of them transvestite "lady boys," stood outside of ping-pong bars waiting for drunk customers to stuff spare bills into their tight miniskirts. If you walked close to them, you could spot traditional jewelry hanging from their ears and necks, often small Buddha figurines made of jade or Chinese eaglewood. They were the ultimate dichotomous offerings; one for the Buddha, one for the belligerent Brit.

I grew tired of bar-hopping and decided to call it a night. I planned to hail a taxi, but once the others yelled sloppy goodbyes to me from the back of motorbikes out front of a bar called Gulliver's Tavern and roared off, I had a sudden change of heart and decided on a whim to walk instead. Almost immediately a couple of young guys catcalled at me from a nearby corner. My cotton tunic clung to my lower back as I began to sweat nervously.

I knew that if I followed the ocean, I would be heading back in the general direction of home. I walked quickly down the main drag, my eyes darting back and forth trying to gain my bearings, my ears catching a mix of pop radio hits and drunken laughter. I considered flagging down a taxi, but I worried that I didn't have enough cash in my coin purse to pay someone a decent amount. It wasn't uncommon for drunk foreigners to be scammed by motorbike drivers, which often led to physical altercations. I thought my best option would be to walk quickly and try to look inconspicuous.

The streetlights grew dimmer as I moved farther out

of town. All I could hear was the click of my plastic ballet flats hitting the uneven pavement as I continued to walk. I'd made it barely a quarter of a mile when I looked down at my watch and saw it was after midnight. I knew my hosts, who had taken a taxi home a good two hours prior, would be wondering where I was. I suddenly became aware of the beads of sweat on my forehead. A surge of anxiety flooded through my body. I tried to avoid looking into the trash-filled alleys I passed, half-lit by the flicker of street lamps. I vaguely recognized a corner market where an elderly woman was hunched over a broom trying to close up shop. She looked up at me, but didn't smile; her face expressed concern in a way that told me, *You shouldn't be here, honey. Get home.* I slung my bag over my shoulder and twisted my now damp hair into a bun. I looked down at my sunburned feet squeezed into my red ballet flats. *These'll have to do*, I thought. I put my head down and began to run.

*   *   *   *   *

I used to hate running. I ran track in sixth grade, but I was not built for it. I played goalie in soccer to avoid the repetitive sprinting required of strikers. I loathed the Wednesday mile run in middle school because my "best" usually landed me somewhere between the middle finishers and dead last. Running was the ultimate social suicide. But when I started my junior year of high school, most of my friends joined the cross country team. I wanted so badly to join my peers on puke-inducing runs in the dead heat of September in Southern California. Although it sounded daunting to run through the barren foothills for seven, eight, up to nine miles right after a long day at school, running seemed to create a sense of community. Suffering brought my friends closer together. Inside jokes about chaffed armpits and naked runs left me feeling excluded.

I started running on the treadmill at our local gym. As a beginner, I wanted to get a sense for what a mile felt like. I ran in an old pair of Asics and my worn track gear, feeling clumsy in my own body as the speed crept up to 6 mph. I felt as if my feet were going to slip off the back of the treadmill. That was if my knees didn't give up first or my tendency for dizziness didn't cause me to fly straight off the back. I watched the time tick slowly, counting the calories as I tried my best to keep one foot in front of the other as gracefully as possible. But lo and behold, I made it to a mile. That was great. So I started to run at the gym as often as I could. Some days would only allow for a ten-minute stint, while some evenings I could run three or four miles without wincing. Eight-hour school days and extracurriculars had me at wit's end, but no matter how tired I was, I motivated myself to at least walk on the treadmill or jog through town.

Running became an essential part of my routine. When I graduated from high school, I spent my graduation gifts on a trip to Europe and visited the Netherlands, Scotland and England. In Liverpool I stayed with a family friend who ran marathons, so I had a partner to show me great running routes. I also found myself unintentionally running while I was abroad. I nearly missed my train to the Amsterdam Schiphol Airport, and as I was running to catch it I found myself nearly keeping pace with it as it pulled into the station. For the record I made it, although sweatier than I had been five minutes earlier. I put my arms up in exhausted victory as I stumbled into the train car.

Traveling and running are similar practices for me. Both require planning and an acute awareness of my surroundings. Both invite the opportunity to escape, but trigger a good amount of anxiety. Both allow me to overcome mental blocks through physical movement. Seeking some direction after my first year of college, I decided to volunteer in Chiang Rai, Thailand, during the summer. Our small cohort of international volunteers worked with the children of northern hill tribe communities, providing them with schooling about cultural preservation, current global events and sustainable farming techniques. I fell in love with my class of sixth graders.

The young monks were quiet and reserved while the others were rambunctious and giggly. They would touch my arm in awe because my skin was so much lighter than their caramel hues. When I walked into the classroom every day, they would squeal in delight yelling, "tee-chah, tee-chah!" They didn't realize it, but I loved seeing their big smiles and crooked teeth, leathered skin and dirty feet. If I let on how easy it was for them to melt my heart, they would have climbed on me like a jungle gym all day and the lessons would never have been completed.

Toward the end of my trip, I fell ill with a fever and chills. Since we were staying so far out in the countryside, my program coordinator decided that just to be sure, an hourlong ride in a rickety tuk-tuk to the nearest hospital was necessary. I wanted to cry. I was shaky and weak and wanted to run away. All I could think about were my parents and how worried they would be to hear I was in the hospital. Here I was, nineteen years old, volunteering in rural Southeast Asia, which my parents allowed me to do only begrudgingly. I dreaded calling them in tears from my death bed to report my case of dysentery or dengue fever.

The doctor saw me right after he stitched up a young Israeli man who had been in a bad motorbike accident. He spoke no English, but he had a funny little chart that showed photos of people with various ailments: a little green man to signify nausea, a little red woman for fever, a crying baby to indicate colic. I pointed to the red woman and showed him the medications I had been taking for the trip, which let him know he could rule out typhoid or malaria. After a blood test and a few exchanges with the nurse, he wrote up a prescription for six medications. I waited in line next to snotty children and shaky elderly monks, feeling at least a little less anxious than I did when I first tried to plan my grand escape from the hospital.

I left the hospital much more content and flagged down a tuk-tuk. The air was sticky and stagnant. The sun was sinking low and seemed to wash the rice paddy fields in a warm sepia hue, taking me back to summer runs I would do back home. The late August warmth enveloped the back of the cab and I stuck my head out of the back to enjoy the breeze on my feverish face. It was as though I were flying: *This is happiness.* Below the hum of the tuk-tuk engine, I heard my driver giggle. He was staring at me in the rear-view mirror. How foolish I must have looked with a grin plastered across my face, a hospital identification tag hanging from my wrist and pouches of expensive medications in my lap. I had to find a way back to this twisted, beautiful country that inspired in me such a deep feeling of euphoric happiness.

So I did. The following March, I finished up my tests early to add a few extra days to spring break. A friend was living in Thailand with her parents, so I invited myself into their home in Pattaya and they told me they would be looking forward to my visit. Heading out of San Francisco Airport, I was nervous and jittery, yearning once again for that sense of complete immersion I had felt months ago in Chiang Rai. Again I was running from the boredom of school.

The first leg of my trip took me to Beijing, and we ended up landing late at night well behind schedule, just fifteen minutes before my connection to Thailand was due to depart. With my fifty-pound backpack and bulky computer bag hanging awkwardly at my side, I ran as fast as I could using moving sidewalks and huffing "Excuse me" to nearly everyone I flew past. I made it to the transfer desk, my face flushed and my chest rising and falling in short, fiery breaths. The woman asked for my passport and stapled a visa to it.

"I'm sorry," I said. "I have a connecting flight. I'm not staying in China."

"Your flight was canceled," she told me. "We have your visa and hotel ready. Next flight to Bangkok tomorrow night."

Her English was clear enough, but dry and emotionless. She stamped my passport and gave me an apathetic smile.

Did she not understand?! I was supposed to be in Bangkok in seven hours. The family I was staying with was sending a driver for me. My roommates would try to contact me. My parents would worry. I had no international phone services. American television stations would report: "Breaking News: Naive University Student Lost in Thick Smog of Beijing." Panic swept over me.

I took my passport from the counter and walked to customs. On top of the complications of entering a communist country, we were the last incoming flight and all 248 of us were delayed. I waited in line two hours before I made it to the train platform that ran from inside the airport to the taxi hub.

About ten of us were transported to the Red Dragon Hotel. The airport personnel had written out our complimentary hotel room vouchers on yellow sticky notes. After much confusion and muffled Chinese between the hotel staff, we were all checked in. I lugged my things up three flights of stairs – the elevator had been "under construction" since the place opened – and lay down to rest.

The next morning, we all caught the southbound train back to the airport. I sat next to a fellow Californian who was finishing grad school at Stanford. We chatted about our travel plans and exchanged playful condolences about college; while he feared post-college adulthood, I dreaded the thousands of dollars in loans I had yet to take out. "I guess I'm running from it," he said.

Two weeks later when I found myself running home from the bar, I realized that what I was running from was myself. In a swell of anxiety and adrenaline, I felt the need to escape something that was bigger than me. My second trip to Thailand was intended to guide me home. At one point during my run I took my shoes off and looped their straps around my wrist. The feeling of warm pavement against my blistered soles was strangely comforting. I imagined myself on the treadmill back home, each foot slapping the rubber at a rhythmic pace as my calves and feet began to burn.

My breath quickened and sweat was now streaming from me. A long bend in the road spit me out onto Soi 16 Street. I had made it. The porch light of the house flickered and a cat groomed herself on the porch. Finally! Winded and drenched, I fumbled to put my key into the lock and open the door as quietly as possible, only to find my friends laughing and drinking in the kitchen.

"Hey! You're so sweaty! Have you been running or something?"

My face flushed with relief.

"Yeah." I took a deep breath. "I'll explain later."

I dropped my bag in the entryway, unburdened finally, and Jacqui handed me a beer.

"Well," she said, "welcome home." She cracked a playful smile and touched her glass to mine.

I fell into the love seat and sighed in relief. "I'll cheers to that."

BONNIE D. FORD, a former sports features writer for the *Chicago Tribune* and *Cleveland Plain Dealer*, is an enterprise and investigative reporter for ESPN.com. She splits her time between suburban Philadelphia and rural Maryland.

BEGINNER'S MIND

BY BONNIE D. FORD

I learned to hate running in a place I otherwise loved: The steep, curving road in suburban Westchester County, New York, where I lived until I was twelve. From the top of that road, I could see across the Hudson River to the very northern end of the Palisades. The profile of those distant hills above a slice of silvery water is as much a part of me as my fingerprints, so I was only mildly surprised when I found out years later that the view included the promontory called High Tor, where my parents went for a picnic the day I was conceived.

We moved into a new two-story colonial at the base of the hill with the wave of other Baby Boom families sweeping into the neighborhood. When I was in fourth and fifth grade, the school bus stopped a few houses away on the flat end of the street. After I graduated to middle school, the stop shifted to the top of the hill. I often was, as I often am now, a few minutes behind schedule, and there was no worse sight than the bright yellow front end of the bus pulling up when I still had half the climb to go.

In my memory, the driver was usually busy watching the kids clambering in on the opposite side and rarely saw me flailing uphill on my stubby legs with my book bag bouncing on my shoulder. My throat and chest would tighten and my lungs would fill shallowly and then empty again with a wheeze like the little bellows we kept on the fireplace. When I didn't make it in time, I faced a two-mile walk to school, the shame of having to stop in the office for a late slip, and the sight of all heads swiveling toward me when I knocked on the classroom door.

I hated running. It made me feel incompetent. Most physical activity did. My mother had noted in my baby book the fact that my left foot flared out slightly (it still does) and the pediatrician's prediction that I would be five-foot-four. As a child, I read those words in her neat cursive hand as if they were runes. I was a dreamy nerd who could conquer almost anything in the classroom but felt doomed to be small and slow and clumsy and near-sighted. I had skipped into first grade halfway through kindergarten, opening up an age gap that accentuated those deficiencies. I was afraid to break my cat-eye glasses. I felt the sting of charity when I was the last one picked for kickball. I couldn't do a single sit-up for the President's Physical Fitness Test when all around me kids were pumping up and down like machines.

The only place I felt at home in my body was in the water. I can't remember learning to swim. I just always knew how. I was never fearful, and I could handle a lot of yardage.

Passing the tests at summer camp came easily to me: Tadpole, Frog, Junior Lifesaver. I swam for the neighborhood club and loved folding double up on the blocks and extending myself into the racing dive. I loved our trips to Jones Beach, where I spent the day diving into the waves and bodysurfing back. Afterward, my bathing suit was always packed with a thick second skin of sand that fell to the ground in chunks when I changed.

Swimming made me weightless and evened out my weaknesses, even though I couldn't see a thing when I took off my glasses. I won the one and only athletic first place of my life the summer I turned twelve in a dual meet against Bedford Golf and Tennis. I went out way too fast in the fifty-yard butterfly and swallowed a lot of water on the back twenty-five, but I heaved my shoulders forward one last time and touched out the girl in the next lane. I can still feel the incredulous smile spreading across my face. The spectators sitting on the grassy slope above the pool looked stunned; they were used to thinking of me as the Kid Who Couldn't.

When I got a little older, I found reasons to run very short distances. I began wearing contact lenses and discovered I could hold my own in stop-and-start sports like basketball and tennis. I cultivated skills that didn't require a great first step. I was a scrappy defensive two-guard with a decent fifteen-foot jumper. I could nail a two-handed backhand down the line. I was a good-field, no-hit sparkplug softball player. Left unguarded in Ultimate Frisbee, I would lurk downfield and relay the occasional bomb pass.

But even a little bit of running often hurt a lot. I was plagued by patellar tendinitis and sprained ankles. After I got out of college, I swore I'd never do it again. My stock line to people was that I couldn't run a mile to save my life. I really believed that.

★ ★ ★ ★ ★

As a sportswriter, I am usually assigned to cover elite athletes, and that is why I had never watched a mass road race finish before the November day I stood in Central Park mesmerized by the sight of amateur runners finishing the 2001 New York City Marathon held two months after 9/11. It was the most magnificent sporting event I'd ever witnessed, a city reasserting itself, the streets flowing with people three and five and eight abreast, running out of defiance and relief and accomplishment, upstaging the still-fresh footage of people fleeing Ground Zero in terror, covered with ash. They streamed by, limping, dancing, in costume, in uniform, in remembrance, in celebration.

I watched, suffused with emotion, and took notes for my column, phrases I hoped would sum up the epic theme before me. But nagging, mundane, selfish thoughts kept darting through my head.

Some of these people are fat! That woman has to be twenty years older than me! That guy is barely lifting his feet! How can these people run 26.2 miles when I can't run a city block?

My job enables me to tap into the fascinating and often freakishly outsized psyches of high-level athletes who burn to win. I've made a living trying to understand their desire and discipline, their failed and successful comebacks, their best impulses and their darker ones, why some choke and others are clutch. Cumulative observation has given me some authority on these matters, but the increment that separates truly extraordinary athletes from the merely excellent remains largely mysterious to me, which is probably what keeps it interesting.

I write about people who make their bodies obey their brains, something I was convinced could never happen for me with my blocked synapses and flat feet. So I got out of the habit of pushing. I'd reach the maximum heart rate listed on whatever machine I happened to be grinding away on – the NordicTrack, the StairMaster, an endless series of recumbent bikes – and back off. I measured my satisfaction by calories burned, laps swum, the digital display on the scale. I dismissed the idea that a PR would ever mean anything to me. I didn't aspire to be in a zone, or out of my comfort zone. It was enough to be mediocre and fit. I drove myself hard enough in other ways.

That day at the NYC Marathon in November 2001 was the first time I'd ever questioned my inability to run. It would take another decade and another tribute to act on it. In those ten years I moved from the city to the suburbs, leaving behind urban bike errands and in-line skating for narrow, unsafe roads and a gym membership. I started a freelance business that kept me at my desk many more hours, got married, was hired by ESPN, traveled more than I ever had. My metabolism slowed and sputtered. My weight, stable since college, crept up a couple pounds a year. What I'd always done wasn't working any more.

Then I started doing interviews for a story about the

2011 New York City Marathon. To commemorate the tenth anniversary of 9/11, the survivors of passengers on Flight 93 – the hijacked jet that crashed in Shanksville, Pennsylvania, detoured by brave civilians determined to abort a suicide mission – had decided to run as a group. I spoke to them on the phone and in their homes in Manhattan and New Jersey and Pennsylvania. Some were already dedicated runners. Many were not. One, the sister-in-law of Jeremy Glick, fell off a treadmill on her first try. Another had crippling knee pain and plantar fasciitis. Several told me they were following a graduated plan, an extended version of couch-to-5K that they downloaded from the Internet.

I stood beyond the finish line and waited for my story subjects. The full range of humanity paraded by in the meantime. A man sagged against the barrier near me and vomited. Two women raised their clasped hands as they passed under the finish banner. All of the Flight 93 runners I'd interviewed made it, some limping in after dusk fell.

I was fond of telling journalism students that elite athletes are wired differently from the rest of us, but these survivors were people like me, other than their horrific and very public losses. My old questions resurfaced, baitfish nibbling my ankles when I swam: *How can all these people run that far when I can't jog longer than thirty seconds? I've reinvented myself professionally and personally several times, so why am I afraid to do this?*

I didn't have to be that kid straining and gasping up the hill, willing the bus not to pull away, fighting tears, embarrassed. No one was watching. I wanted to be able to run a mile. Then I'd see.

* * * * *

I started in September on the deserted soccer fields in my neighborhood, running down the out-of-bounds line for a minute, then ninety seconds, then around the perimeter, counting the steps hyperconsciously, fighting my inner-child feelings of foolishness. At our family home in rural Maryland, I walked down the 250-yard gravel driveway to the road and ran back up the stripe of dirt and grass in the middle and then repeated, feeling the slight incline, stopping for water often in the lingering heat of early fall.

I feared running on asphalt, feared getting hurt and losing my resolve and momentum. My knees held up - I told myself they were twenty years younger than my biological age, since I'd spared them until now - but my shins balked and ached. I babied myself with heating pads and ice after every little workout.

Soon enough, the weather got colder and I moved inside and began running at night, on the indoor track at my gym. It was slightly banked, with a good springy surface, one-fifth of a mile, and encircled a cluster of tennis courts in the middle. These were ringed by rubber curtains so I couldn't see the other side of the track and think about how far away it was. That was key.

I am the antithesis of a morning person, and working out late always made sense to me – un-kinking from a long day at my desk, working through a reporting or writing problem in the pool or on the elliptical machine. I soon began to recognize regulars in the small group of night runners. There were women or couples who power-walked side by side, a boy who ran with his father. There were high school and college students who floated by, moving fluidly, their swinging ponytails and the backs of their calves taunting me as they disappeared around the curve. I felt envy that bordered on anger: It had never been that easy for me.

The most distinctive regular was an older man who wore a back brace and what looked like ankle weights. He leaned awkwardly forward as he trundled along and appeared to my unpracticed eye as if he were doing absolutely everything wrong. But in a paradigm by now very familiar to me, he could run a lot farther than I could. At random intervals he let out a howl that in its groaning intensity could have been mistaken for someone crying out in the heat of passion. The first time I heard him as he steamed up behind me, I hopped off the track in alarm, thinking he'd injured himself.

I gradually built up to a whole lap and then another, and my total distance climbed to two or three miles, with breaks to walk. The air was dry and foul-smelling and the airplane-hangar enclosure got cold in the winter, so I used my asthma inhaler and started my workouts in a jacket and scarf, stripping as I went along. I began to feel ownership of the crazy little ecosystem and its etiquette. When kids spilled out of a tennis lesson and began walking the wrong way around the track, I yelled at them.

I still counted and begrudged most of my steps. I felt no runner's high. It was hard every time. I tried, both consciously and unconsciously, to distract myself. I wrote part of a song in my head; I pictured someone I knew ahead of me on the track, around the corner, waiting to encourage me. My mind would drift for just a few seconds to something other than my discomfort – an issue at work, a pleasant memory – then yank me back to full awareness of what I was doing. Those moments were little moral victories and defeats all at once, with a frustrating, involuntary sense of having had a good dream interrupted.

My legs got stronger and I no longer needed to ice after every session. My resolve also hardened. For the first time in a nomadic career devoted to dissecting the sources of other people's athletic motivation, I found my own.

As I walked a wide, deserted beach at low tide on the Oregon coast, calming myself after hearing upsetting news, I felt water seeping around my toes and realized I was wearing running shoes. So I ran to exorcise my worry, reveling in the perfect surface of hard-packed sand painted pastel shades by the sunset's reflection.

I sat in a carpeted room in Connecticut and interviewed marathon world record holder Paula Radcliffe, who'd been hobbled by foot surgery. I took notes as she described "shuffle-jogging" to get herself moving again. I thought, *if she can humble herself that way, why should I be sheepish?*

I reported from Boston during and after the bombings at the marathon and afterward used gratitude to talk myself through some runs: *Run because you can. Run because it's a privilege. You have both legs.*

I ran a mile continuously for the first time on a treadmill in a hotel fitness room in Toronto and raised my arms, all alone in my modest triumph. It was self-mocking and dead serious at the same time. I'd been wrong in my old self-deprecating declaration. As it turned out, running a mile was one way to save my life – my emotional life as much as my physical health.

The fact that I couldn't excel made running all the more appealing. I didn't like doing it but I loved the way it made me feel afterwards, an unfamiliar sore and taut that told me my body was learning something new. I am not happy unless I'm pushing back against history and preconceived notions, keeping my mind and heart open to possibility. Learning to run from scratch was a way to retain the muscle memory of being young, when it was natural to embrace surprise, take a blind corner and let myself fall for something I couldn't have seen coming.

* * * * *

I told very few people when I started to run. I was too afraid I would fail and I didn't want to be asked about it months later. Now that I know I can do it, I still have no desire to enter a race. The thought of running in a crowd gives me claustrophobia and I am stubborn in my conviction that my particular goal does not require a finish line. I still swim and bike and skate and kayak and paddleboard and do yoga. The difference now is that I know I will always mix in a little running. I'd like to be able to run three miles. Then I'll see.

Early one evening, I ventured outdoors to the high school track in my neighborhood. The infield was empty and I could see the whole brick-colored oval yawning before me. I stretched a little and put my aluminum water bottle on a bench and hop-stepped into a run. *You don't need to go fast,* I reminded myself. *No one is watching. You are not going to be late.*

I plodded by a coach tutoring a brace of kids on start technique. Ambient noise from a nearby soccer practice wafted to me on the breeze, briefly taking me away from what I'd been doing until my obstinate mind yanked me back again. A woman in her twenties passed me, sweat-stains darkening her chest and back, running easier than I ever had or would. I felt my old envy sizzle and evaporate like water dribbled on a hot pan. I kept going. I passed the quarter-mile mark, rounded the first curve again and caught an odd movement in my peripheral vision. It flickered to my right and then ahead of me, indecipherable for a few seconds. Then it heaved into view and I realized it was my own shadow: my head and shoulders and torso and my arms pumping over elongated legs. I smiled, incredulous, and watched for a few strides before I lifted my chin and looked ahead again.

ABOUT WELLSTONE BOOKS

We are an independent publisher in Northern California
that focuses on personal writing that is not afraid to inspire.
We believe that changes in the publishing landscape create an
opening for small publishers committed to developing each
project as a labor of love, and we insist on taking the time to
let a manuscript develop with care and consideration. Our
experienced team brings decades of experience to editing and
design, and our titles have received coverage in publications
ranging from the *San Francisco Chronicle* and *San Jose Mercury
News* to the *New York Times* and New Yorker.com, as well as
cracking regional bestseller lists. We do not accept unsolicited
manuscripts, but are always looking for writers who are familiar
with our publishing philosophy and want to work with us to
develop future projects. Interested writers, or journalists in search
of review copies or author availability, write to:

books@wellstoneredwoods.org

WELLSTONE CENTER
in the Redwoods

The Wellstone Center in the Redwoods, a writer's retreat center in Northern California, publishes books under its Wellstone Books imprint and offers weeklong writing residencies, monthlong writing fellowships and occasional weekend writing workshops; we also host regular Author Talk events. Founded by Sarah Ringler and Steve Kettmann, WCR has been hailed in the *San Jose Mercury News* as a beautiful, inspiring environment that is "kind of like heaven" for writers, described in the *San Francisco Chronicle* as "the kind of place where inspiration seems to just hang in the air, waiting to be inhaled," and featured in *San Francisco Magazine*'s "Best of the Bay" issue. Visit our website at **www.wellstoneredwoods.org** for the latest on our programs.

A special thanks to each of the contributors to this *Night Running* collection, who donated their essays without compensation in support of our programs for writers at WCR. In gratitude we offer each of the writers a one-week writing residency here in our peaceful enclave low in the Santa Cruz Mountains. We're putting together a *Night Running 2* collection; writers interested in contributing should email us at **info@wellstoneredwoods.org** for guidelines.

ALSO AVAILABLE FROM WELLSTONE BOOKS

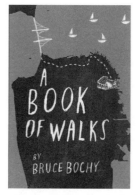

A Book of Walks
BY BRUCE BOCHY

The manager of the San Francisco Giants, having taken his team to World Series victories in 2010, 2012 and 2014, is known nationally for his rare knack for staying on an even keel even in the midst of some very stressful situations. How does he do it? One thing he's always tried to do is get in regular long walks, which help him clear his head and get over the disappointments of the day. This pocket-sized volume, dubbed "an endearing little book" by the *New York Times*, takes us with Bochy on eight talks around the country, each its own chapter (complete with map of his route). Come along for the ride on walks through Central Park in New York, along Lake Michigan in Chicago and across San Francisco to the Golden Gate Bridge. How does Bochy keep a cool head, the Toronto *Globe and Mail* asked?

"In the tradition of thinkers like Rousseau, Kant and Thoreau, Bochy, sixty, swears by long strolls and vigorous walks – 'the freedom to be alone with my thoughts for a while' – which he makes time for wherever he is," Nathalie Atkinson writes.

A Book of Walks, a Northern California bestseller, makes a memorable gift for any baseball fan – or fan of walks.

Kiss the Sky: My Weekend in Monterey at the Greatest Concert Ever
By Dusty Baker

For his eighteenth birthday, Dusty Baker's mother gave him a great present: Two tickets to the Monterey Pop Festival of June 1967, a three-day event featuring more than thirty bands, and use of the family station wagon for the weekend so young Dusty could drive down from Sacramento to the Monterey Bay. He was another young person, trying to take it all in, sleeping on the beach with his buddy, having the time of his life soaking up the vibe and every different musical style represented there. Baker's lifelong love of music was set in motion, his wide-ranging, eclectic tastes, everything from country to hip-hop. He also caught the Jimi Hendrix Experience, who put on such a show that to this day Baker calls Hendrix the most exciting performer he's ever seen. He went on to years of friendship with musicians from B.B. King and John Lee Hooker to Elvin Bishop. This account grabs a reader from page one and never lets up.

"At its best, the book evokes not only the pleasure of music, but the connection between that experience and the joy of sports," NewYorker. com writes.

"Reading *Kiss the Sky* is like having a deep conversation with Dusty Baker – about baseball, fathers and sons, race, culture, family, religion, politics – and always music," says Joan Walsh of MSNBC. "He doesn't sugarcoat anything, but he makes you feel good about being alive nonetheless."

#1 in Wellstone Books' "Music That Changed My Life" series.

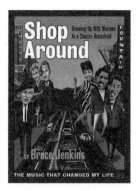

Shop Around: Growing Up With Motown in a Sinatra Household

By Bruce Jenkins

Bruce Jenkins was twelve years old, living in Malibu with his parents, when he heard the original "Shop Around" single, by "The Miracles featuring Bill 'Smokey' Robinson," the first Billboard No. 1 R&B single for Motown's Tamla label. Released nationally in October 1960, the single would ultimately make it into the Grammy Hall of Fame, and for young Bruce, it was a revelation. Jenkins grew up surrounded by music. His father, Gordon Jenkins, was a composer and arranger who worked with artists from Ella Fitzgerald and Billie Holiday to Louis Armstrong and Johnny Cash, but was best known for his close collaboration with Frank Sinatra. His mother, Beverly, was a singer. For Bruce, "Shop Around" ushered him into a new world of loving Motown. In *Shop Around*, he brings to life the first thrill of having the music claim him, sketches from his life with his father and mother, and traces how his love of music has grown and evolved over the years.

"Bruce Jenkins manages to accomplish the always dangerous task of describing music with words as well as anyone I've read," rocker Huey Lewis says. "His knowledge is formidable and his passion is infectious.

"A warm and witty memoir about how music binds us all," according to Joel Selvin, *San Francisco Chronicle* pop music critic.

"An absolutely essential read. An awesome story about a priceless time in music history," adds Emilio Castillo, Bandleader for Tower of Power.

#2 in Wellstone Books' "Music That Changed My Life" series.